RECORDED VERSIONS
GUITAR

AUTHENTIC TRANSCRIPTIONS
WITH NOTES AND TABLATURE

ROCK BAND™

ISBN 978-1-4234-3429-0

HAL•LEONARD®
CORPORATION
7777 W. BLUEMOUND RD. P.O. BOX 13819 MILWAUKEE, WI 53213

Visit Hal Leonard Online at
www.halleonard.com

ROCKBAND

Are You Gonna Be My Girl

Words and Music by Nic Cester and Cameron Muncey

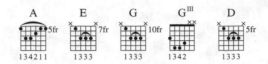

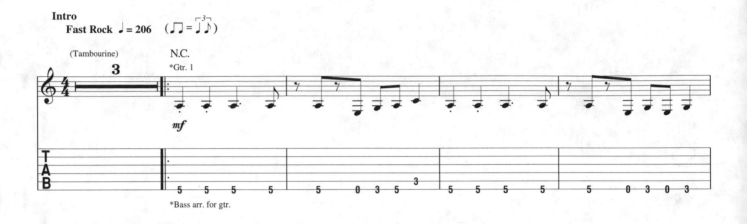

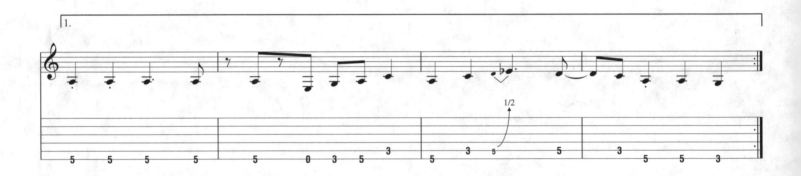

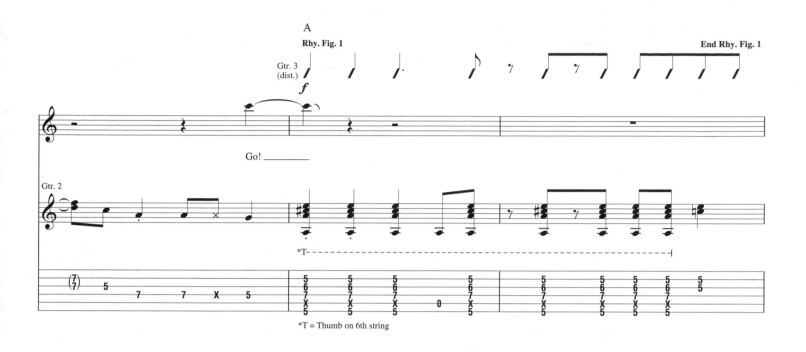

*T = Thumb on 6th string

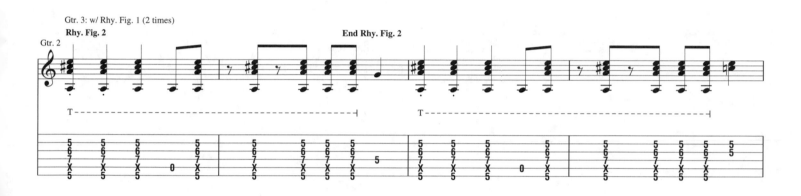

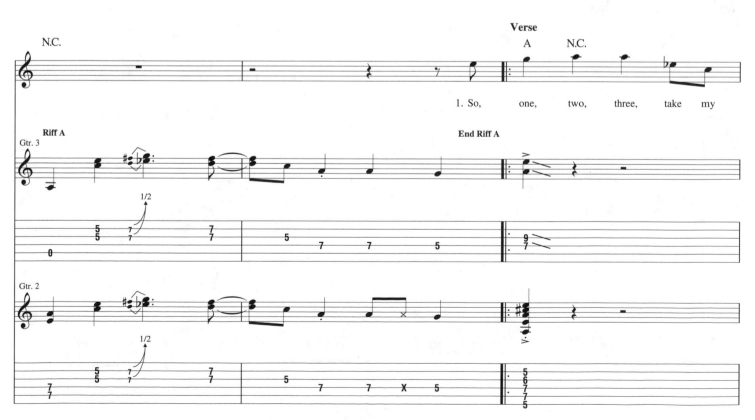

Gtrs. 2 & 3 tacet

hand and come with me be-cause you look so fine and I real-ly want to make you mine.

Gtr. 3: w/ Rhy. Fig. 1

I say you look so fine and I real-ly want to make you mine.

Gtr. 3: w/ Rhy. Fig. 1

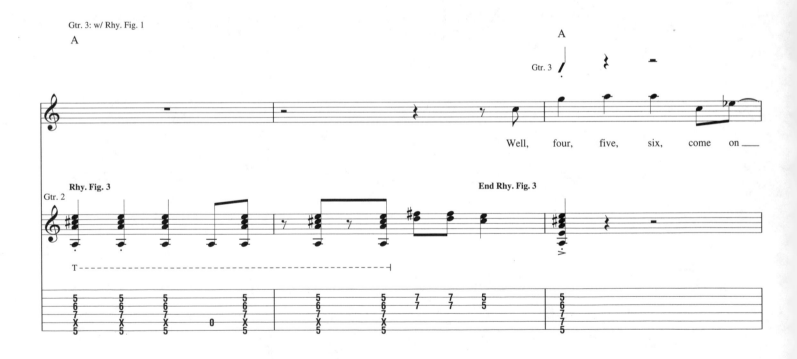

Well, four, five, six, come on ___

Gtrs. 2 & 3 tacet

___ and get your kicks. Now you don't need mon-ey { when you look like that, do you, hon-ey? / with a face like that, do ya? ___ }

Gtr. 3: w/ Rhy. Fig. 1

Gtr. 3: w/ Riff A

N.C.

Gtr. 2

Pre-Chorus

Gtrs. 2 & 3: w/ Rhy. Fig. 4 (2 times)

Big ___ black boots, long ___ brown hair. ___

Rhy. Fig. 4

End Rhy. Fig. 4

**Gtrs. 2 & 3

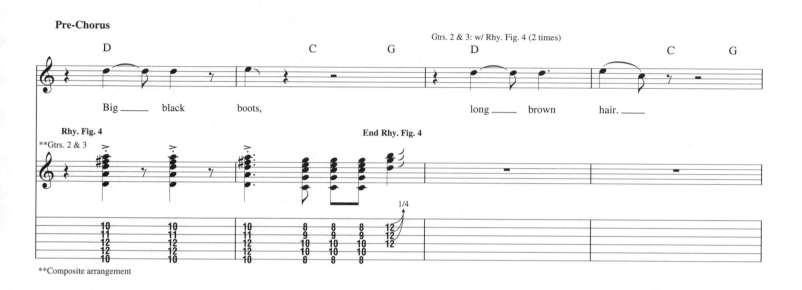

**Composite arrangement

She's ___ so sweet with ___ her get ___ back stare.

Gtrs. 2 & 3

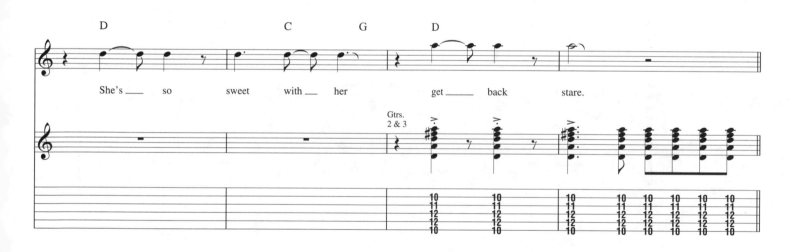

Chorus

Well, I could see ___ you home with me, ___

Rhy. Fig. 5

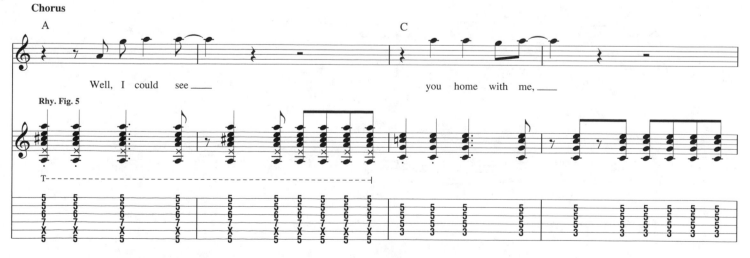

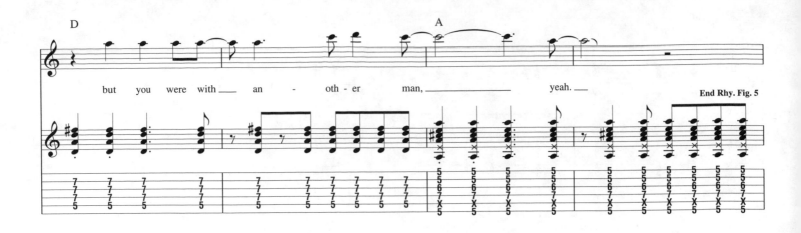

but you were with ___ an - oth - er man, ___ yeah. ___

End Rhy. Fig. 5

Gtrs. 2 & 3: w/ Rhy. Fig. 5

I ___ know we ain't ___ got much to say ___

be - fore I let ___ you get a - way, ___ yeah. ___

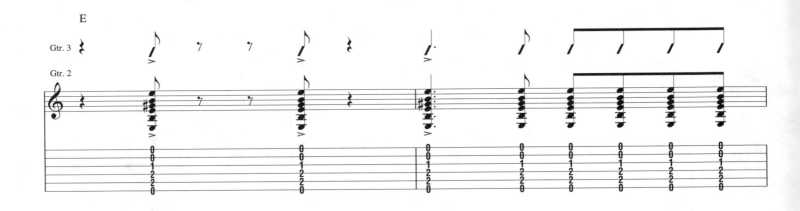

Gtr. 3

Gtr. 2

1.

I said, "Are you gon - na be my girl?" ___

8

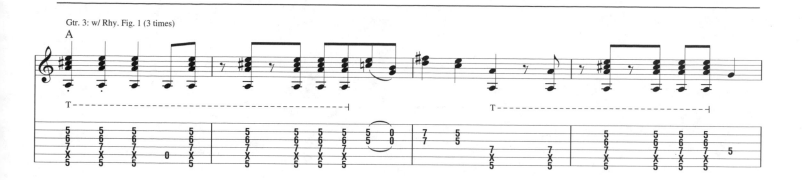

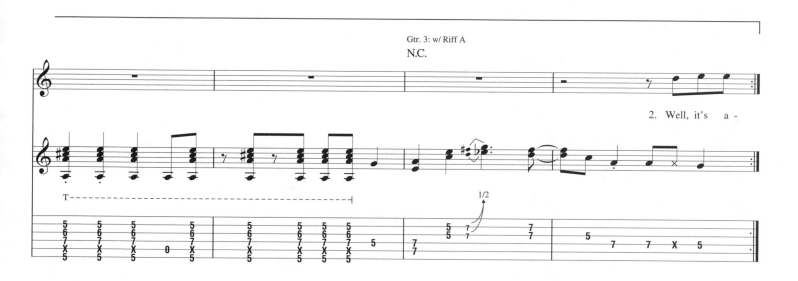

Ah,

Guitar Solo

Gtr. 2: w/ Rhy. Fig. 2 (4 times)

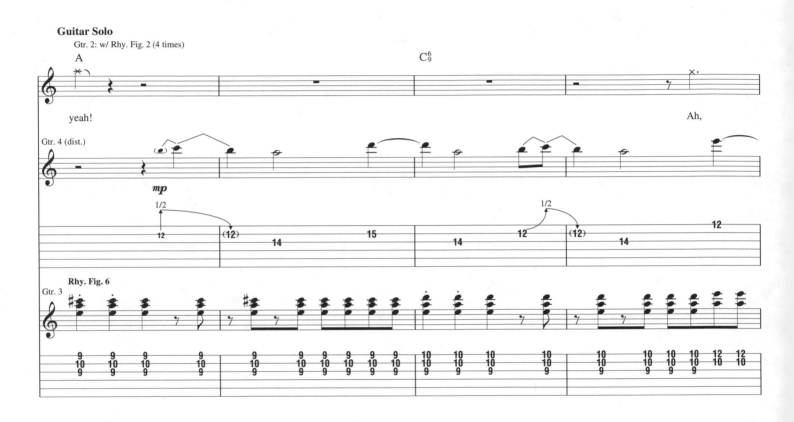

yeah!

Ah,

Rhy. Fig. 6

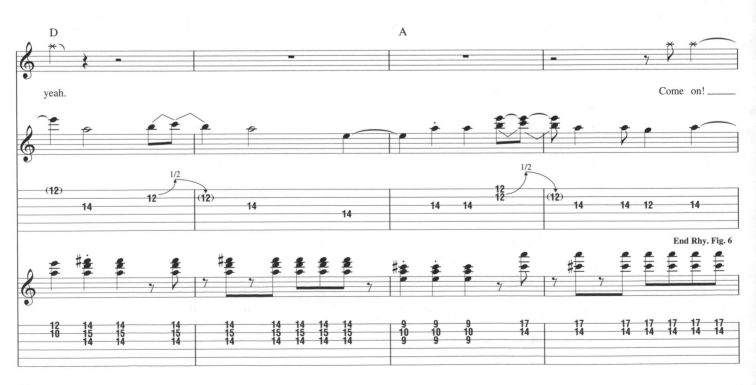

yeah.

Come on! ____

End Rhy. Fig. 6

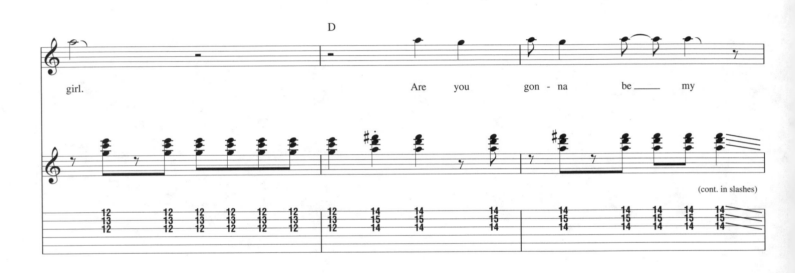

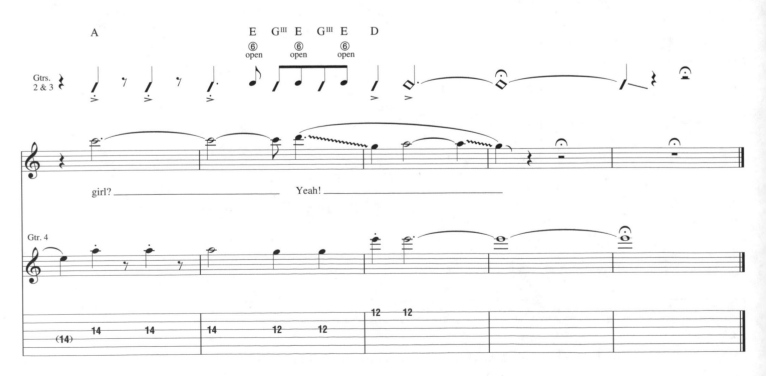

Black Hole Sun

Words and Music by Chris Cornell

*Drop D Tuning:
① = E ④ = D
② = B ⑤ = A
③ = G ⑥ = D
*All gtrs. sound 1/4 step sharp

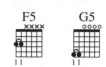

F5   G5

Intro
Slow Rock ♩ = 52

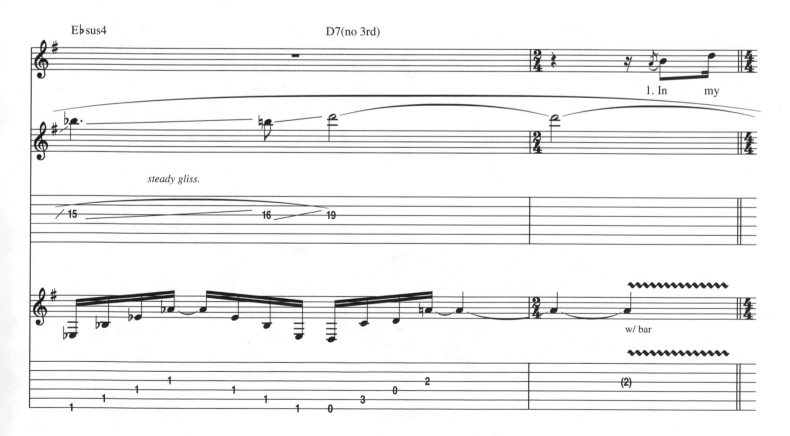

eyes, ___ in - dis - posed, in dis - guise as no ___ one knows, ___ hides the face, ___

2. See Additional Lyrics

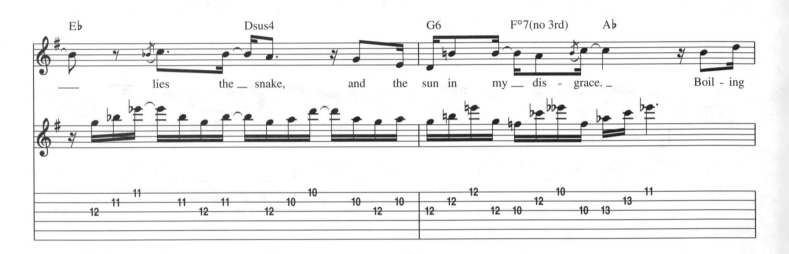

___ ___ lies the ___ snake, and the sun in my ___ dis - grace. ___ Boil - ing

heat, ___ sum - mer stench. ___ 'Neath the black, the sky ___ looks dead. ___ Call my name ___

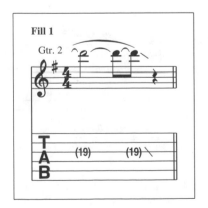

Fill 1

14

Additional Lyrics

2. Stuttering, cold and damp.
   Steal the warm wind, tired friend.
   Times are gone for honest men,
   And sometimes far too long for snakes.
   In my shoes, a walking sleep.
   In my youth I pray to keep.
   Heaven send hell away.
   No one sings like you anymore.

Creep

**Words and Music by Albert Hammond, Mike Hazlewood, Thomas Yorke,
Richard Greenwood, Philip Selway, Colin Greenwood and Edward O'Brian**

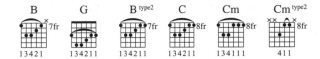

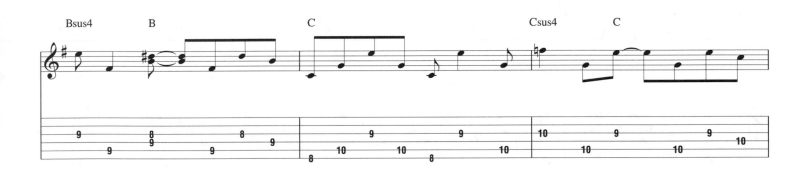

1. When you were here _ be - fore, ___

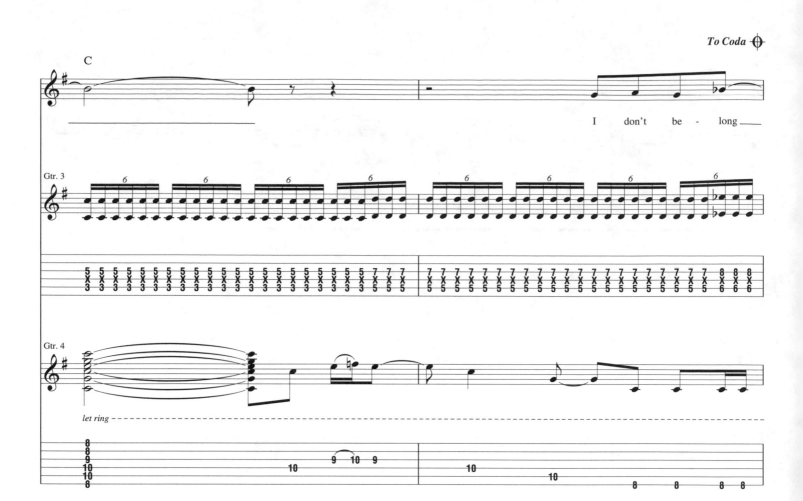

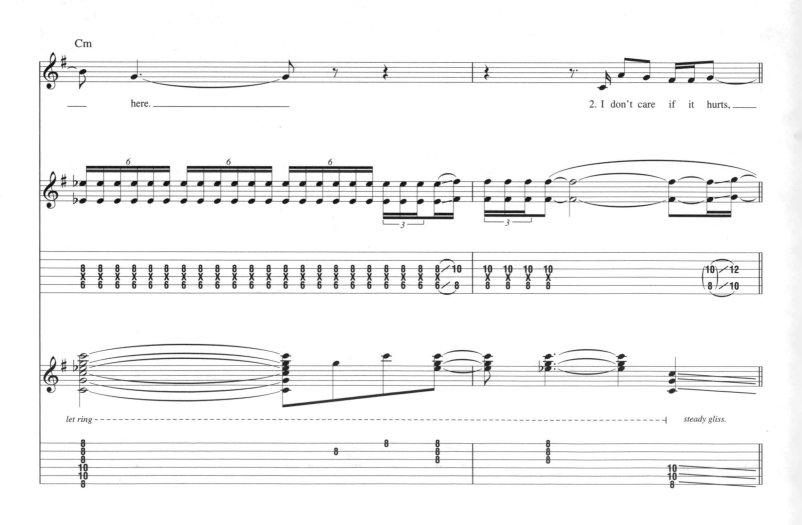

Verse

I wan-na have con-trol.

I want a per-fect bod - y. I want a per-fect soul.

I want you to no - tice when I'm not a - round.

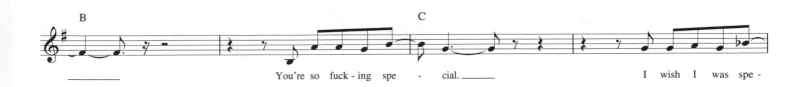

You're so fuck-ing spe - cial. I wish I was spe-

*Microphonic fdbk, not caused by string vibration.

⊕ Coda

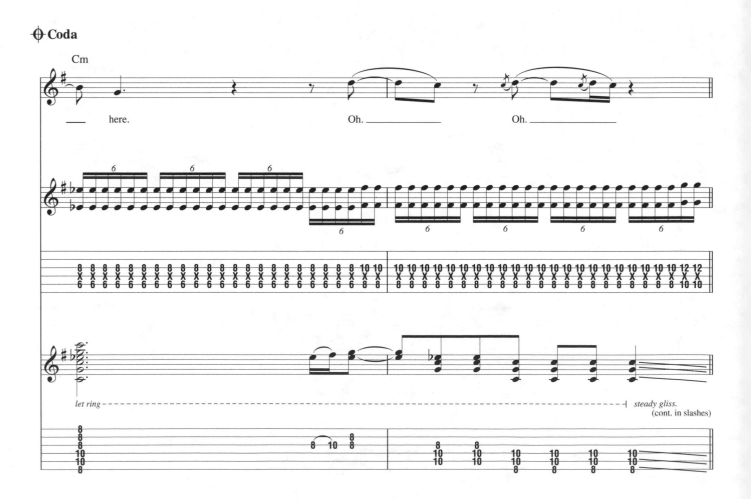

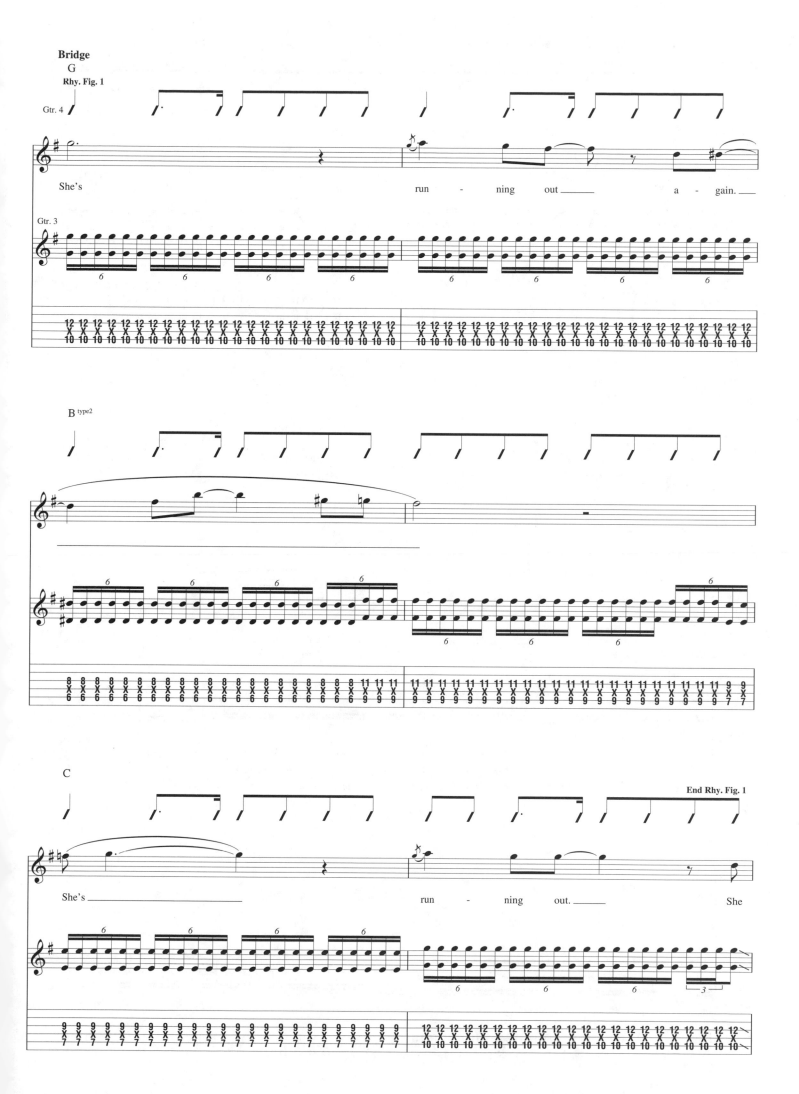

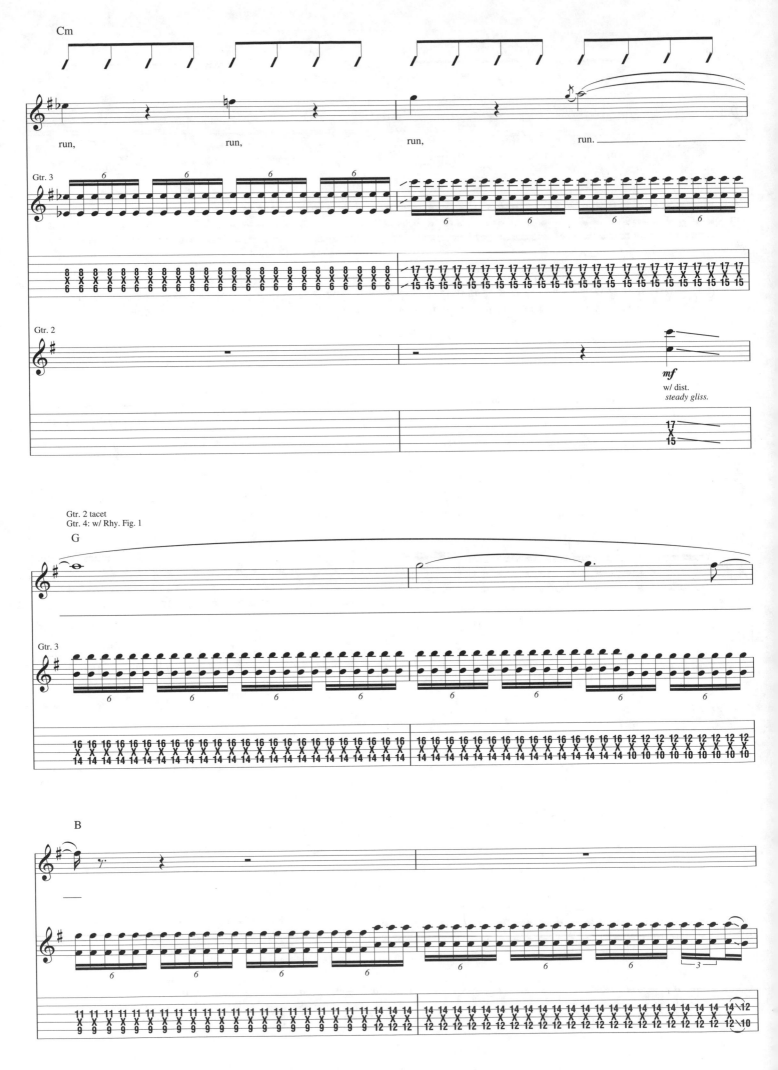

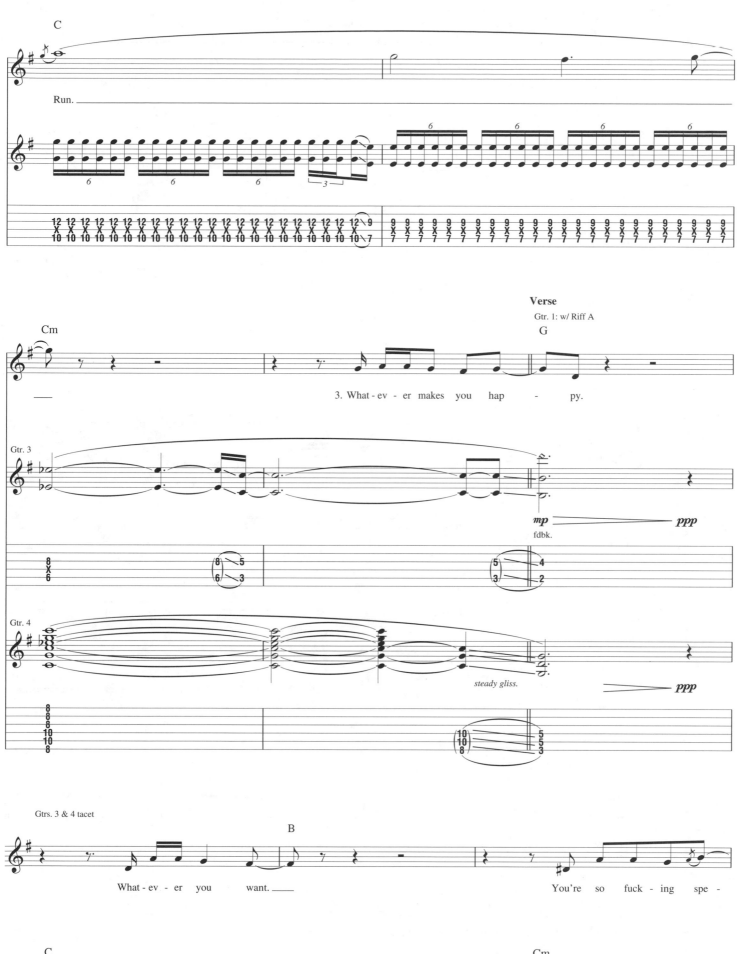

Outro-Chorus

Gtr. 1: w/ Riff B (1st 6 meas.)

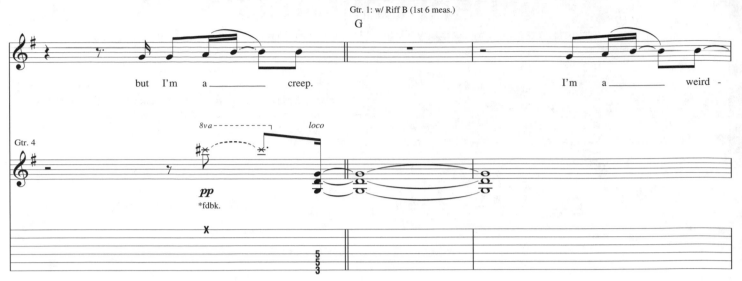

but I'm a _____ creep. I'm a _____ weird-

*Microphonic fdbk., not caused by string vibration.

-o. _____ What the hell am I do-ing here? ___

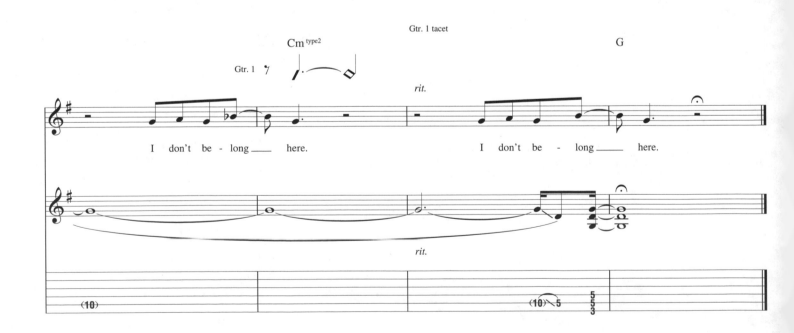

I don't be-long ___ here. I don't be-long ___ here.

Dani California

Words and Music by Anthony Kiedis, Flea, John Frusciante and Chad Smith

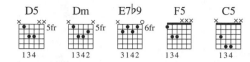

Intro
Moderately ♩ = 96

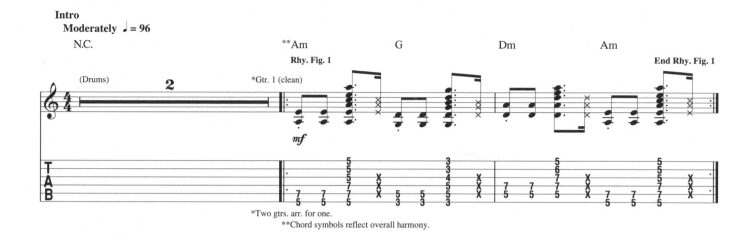

*Two gtrs. arr. for one.
**Chord symbols reflect overall harmony.

Verse
Gtr. 1: w/ Rhy. Fig. 1 (2 times)

1. Get-ting born ___ in the state of Mis-sis-sip-pi, pa - pa was a cop-per and her ma-ma was a hip-pie.

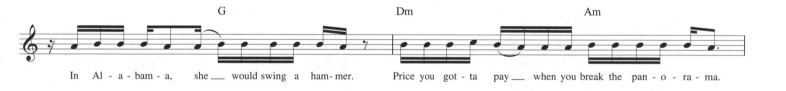

In Al-a-bam-a, she ___ would swing a ham-mer. Price you got-ta pay ___ when you break the pan-o-ra-ma.

She nev-er knew that there was an-y-thing more ___ than poor.

w/ modular filter

***Gtr. 2 (clean), *mf* Composite arrangement

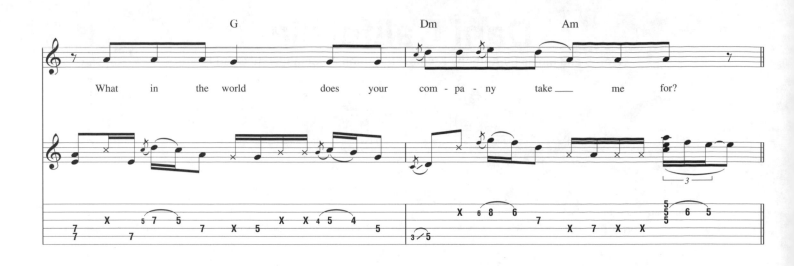

What in the world does your com-pa-ny take me for?

Verse

*Gtr. 1: w/ Rhy. Fig. 1 (2 times)

Gtr. 2 tacet

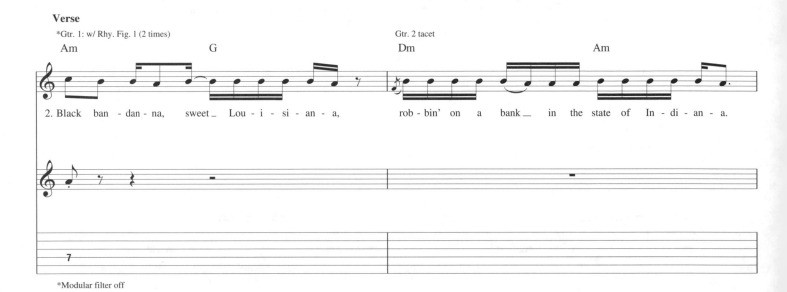

2. Black ban-dan-na, sweet Lou-i-si-an-a, rob-bin' on a bank in the state of In-di-an-a.

*Modular filter off

She's a run-ner, reb-el, and a stun-ner, on her mer-ry way, say-in', "Ba-by, what-cha gon-na?"

**Gtrs. 1 & 2

Riff A

End Riff A

Look-ing down the bar-rel of a hot met-al for-ty-five. Just an-oth-er way to sur-vive.

w/ modular filter

**Composite arrangement

Lyrics under the music:

3. She's a lov-er, ba - by, and a fight-er. Should-a seen her com-in' when it got a lit-tle bright-er.

With a name like Dan - i Cal-i-for-nia, (the) day ____ was gon-na come ____ when I ____ was gon-na mourne ____ ya.

Too true to say, _____ say, _____ say...

Verse

Gtr. 1: w/ Rhy. Fig. 1 (2 times)

4. Push the fad - er, gift - ed an - i - ma - tor one _____ for the now _____ and e - lev - en for the lat - er.

Nev - er made it up _____ to Min - ne - so - ta, North Da - ko - ta man _____ was a gun - nin' for the quo - ta.

Down in the Bad - lands, she was sav - in' the best ___ for last. It on - ly hurts when I laugh. ___

*w/ modular filter

D.S. al Coda 2

Gone ___ too fast. ___ Cal - i - for -

***Gtrs. 10, 11 & 12

†w/ dist. & octaver

***Three gtrs., each playing single notes

†Octaver set for one octave above
to simulate sped-up gtrs.

**Gtrs. 7, 8 & 9

w/ dist.

**Three gtrs., each playing single notes

Gtr. 2

Gtr. 3

††Vol. swell

*w/ flanger on entire mix

Outro-Guitar Solo

Detroit Rock City

Words and Music by Paul Stanley and Bob Ezrin

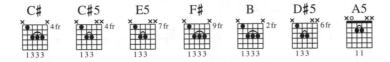

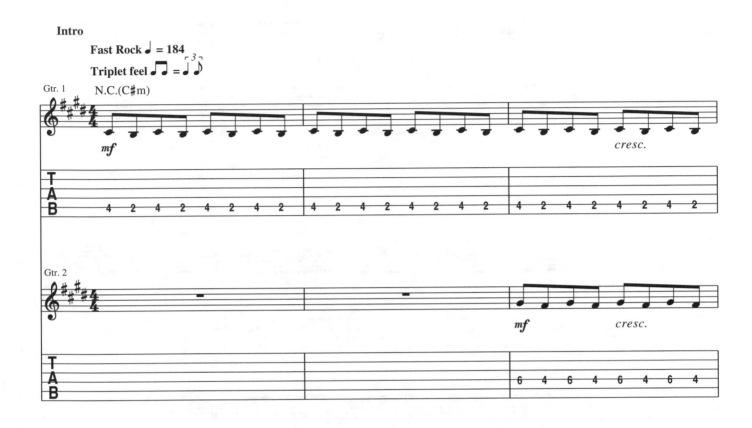

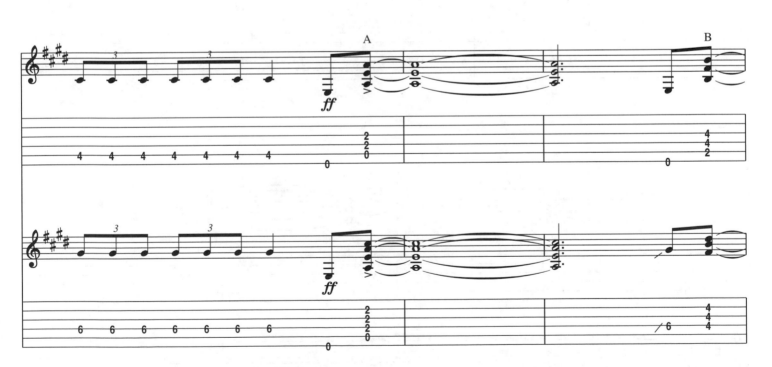

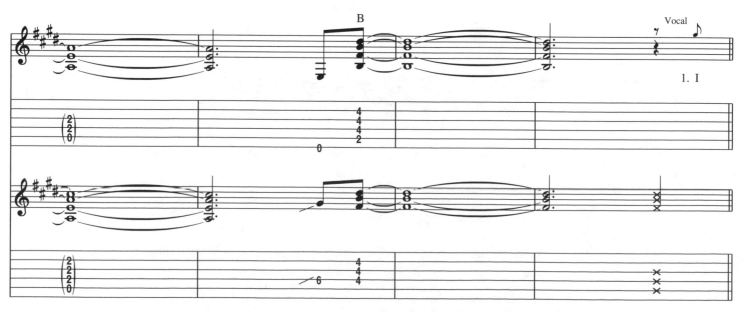

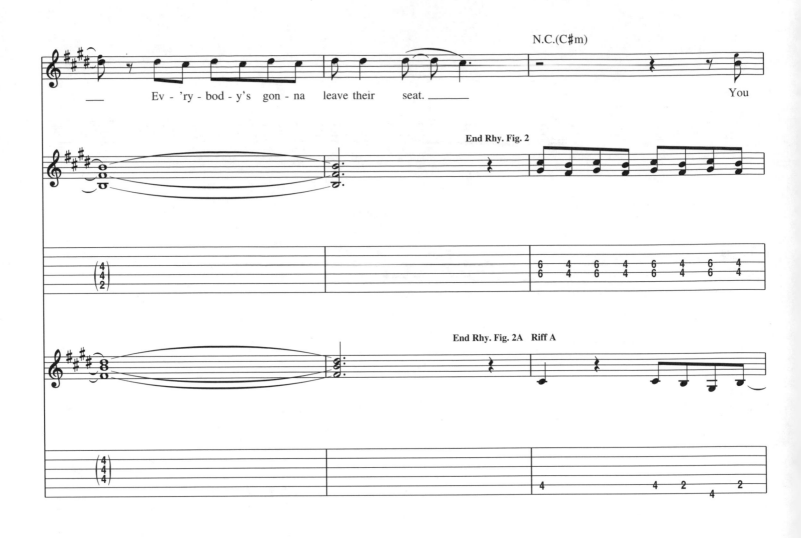

Ev - 'ry - bod - y's gon - na leave their seat. _____

You

got - ta lose your mind in De - troit Rock Cit - y. Get up! _

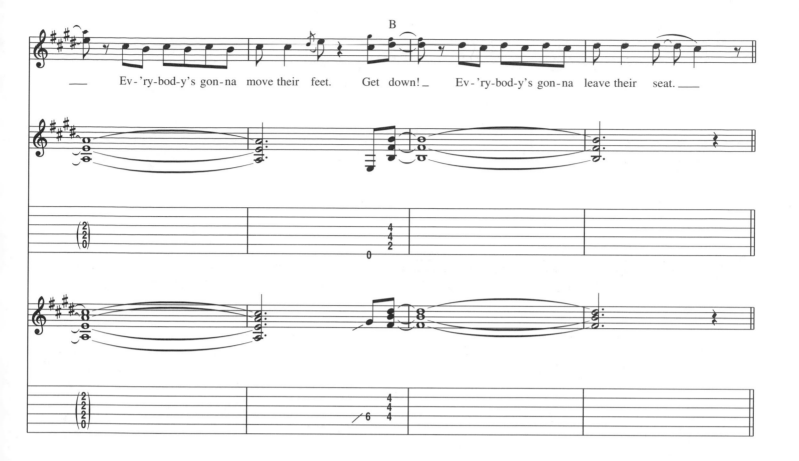

Ev-'ry-bod-y's gon-na move their feet. Get down! Ev-'ry-bod-y's gon-na leave their seat.

Verse

Gtrs. 1 & 2: w/Rhy. Fig. 1

2. Get-tin' late, I just can't wait. Ten o'-clock, and I

know I got-ta hit the road. First I drink, then I smoke.

Start up the car, and I try to make the mid-night show. Get up!

Chorus

Gtr. 1: w/Rhy. Fig. 2
Gtr. 2: w/Rhy. Fig. 2A

Ev-'ry-bod-y's gon-na move their feet. Get down! Ev-'ry-bod-y's gon-na leave their seat.

feel so good; I'm so a-live. __ Hear my song __

play-in' on the ra-di-o._____ It goes: _ Get up! __ Ev-'ry-bod-y's gon-na

move their feet. Get down! _ Ev-'ry-bod-y's gon-na leave their seat. _____

You got - ta lose your life in De - troit Rock Cit - y.

Gtr. 2: w/Rhy. Fig. 2A

Verse

Gtr. 1 & 2: w/Rhy. Fig. 1

4. Twelve o' - clock, _ I got - ta rock. _ There's a

truck a - head, _ lights star - in' at my eyes. _____

Whoa, my god, _ no time to turn. _ I got to laugh _ 'cause I

Chorus

Gtrs. 1 & 2: w/Rhy. Fig. 2 & 2A

know I'm gon - na die. ___ Why? ___ Get up! ___ Ev - 'ry - bod - y's gon - na

move their feet. _____ (Get down!) __

Gtr. 3

Gtr. 4

Gtrs. 1 & 2

A5

(Drum fill)

2

Get up! _____ Ev - 'ry - bod - y's gon - na

leave their seat, _____ get down! __

E   B

G#   C#

Gtr. 3

8va

Gtr. 4

Fill 1
Gtrs. 1 & 2

Don't Fear the Reaper

Words and Music by Donald Roeser

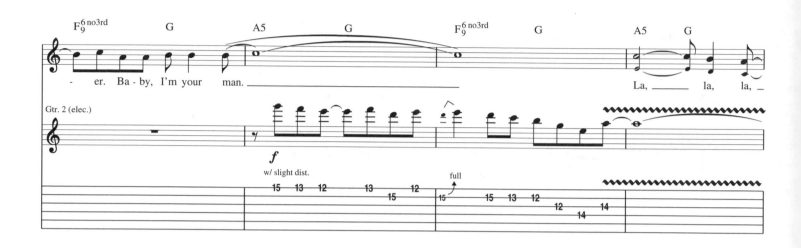

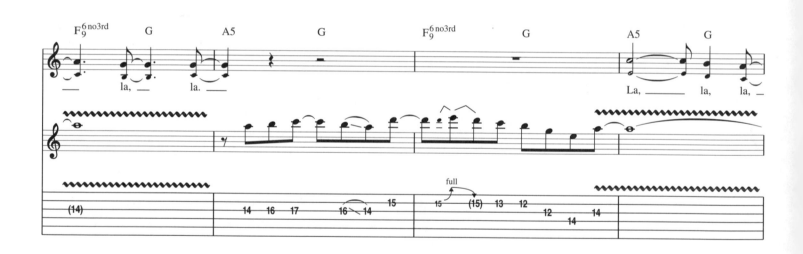

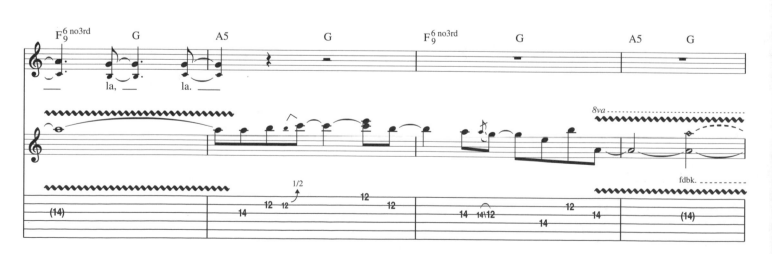

50

Verse

2. Val - en - tine _____ is _____ done. _____

Here _____ but now _____ they're _ gone. _____

Chorus

Ro - me - o and Ju - li - et _____ are to - geth - er in e - ter - ni - ty. _____

(Rom - e - o and Ju -

For - ty thou - sand men and wom - en ev - 'ry day.

- li - et.)

(Like Rom - e - o and Ju - li - et.)

For - ty thou - sand men and wom - en ev -

-'ry day. A - noth-er for - ty thou-sand com-ing ev - 'ry day.
(Re - de - fine hap - pi - ness.) (We can be like they _

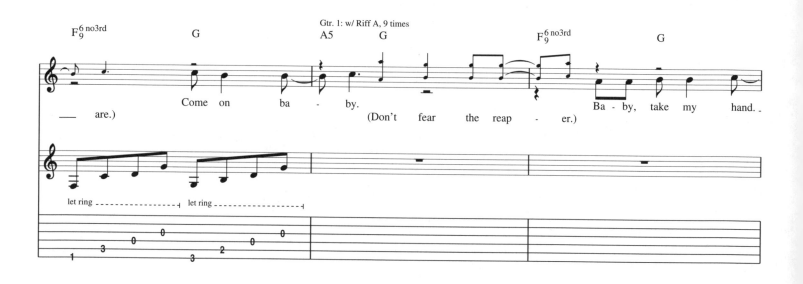

Gtr. 1: w/ Riff A, 9 times

_ are.) Come on ba - by. (Don't fear the reap - er.) Ba - by, take my hand. _

_ (Don't fear the reap - er.) We'll be a - ble to fly. ____ (Don't fear the reap -

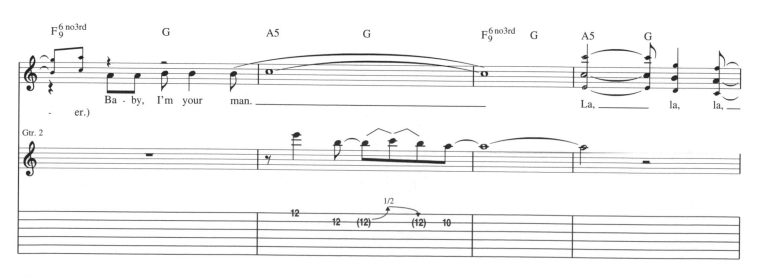

Ba - by, I'm your man. ____ La, _____ la, la, _

- er.)

Gtr. 2

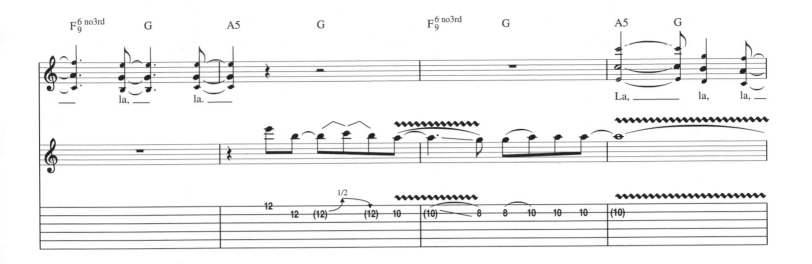

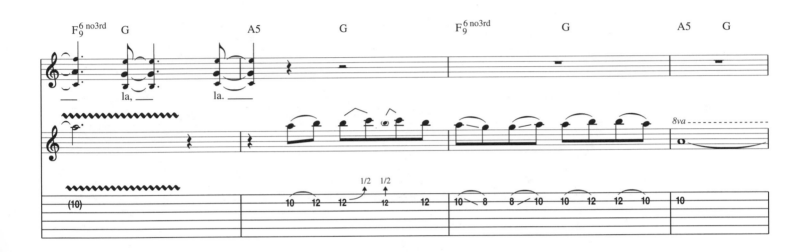

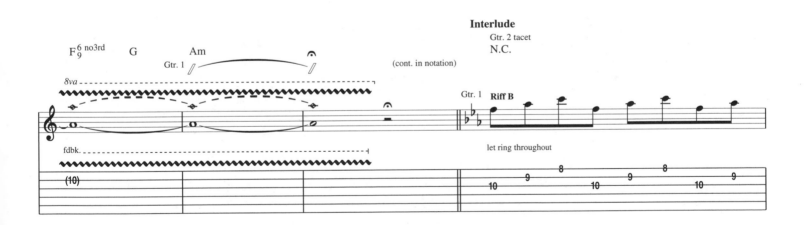

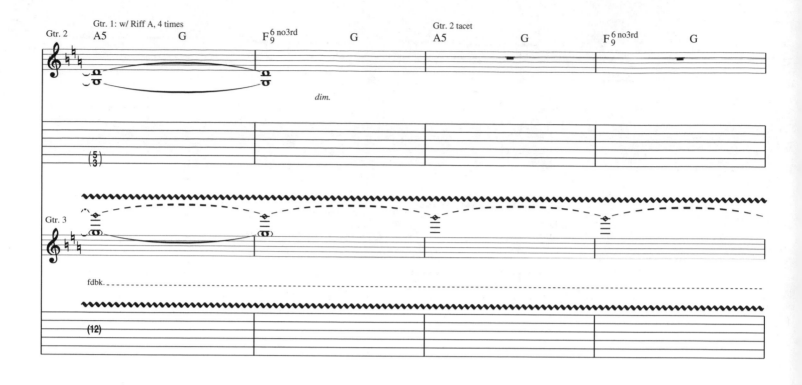

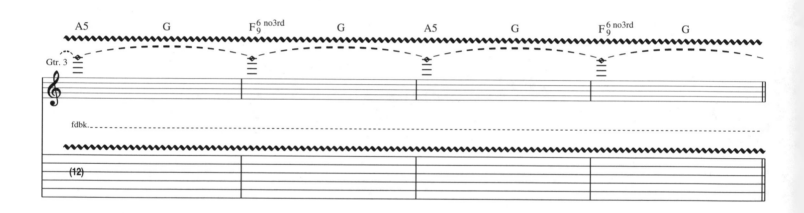

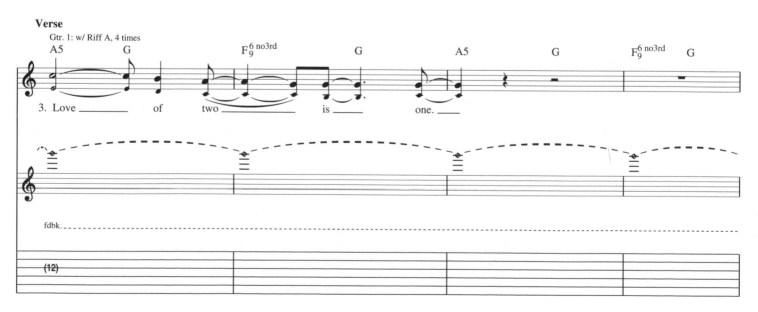

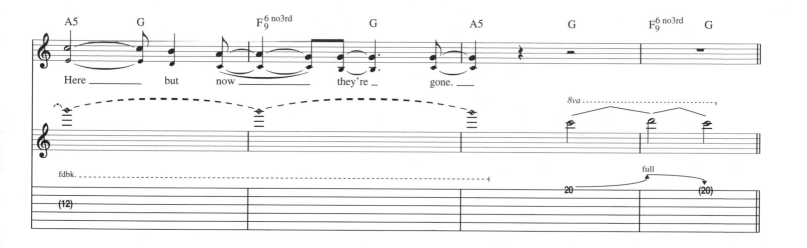

Here ___ but now ___ they're ___ gone. ___

Chorus

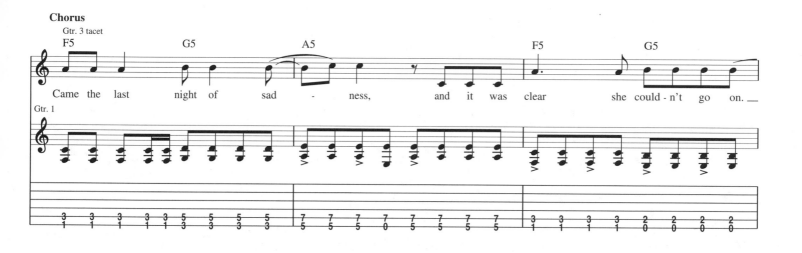

Came the last night of sad - ness, and it was clear she could - n't go on. ___

— And the door was o - pen and the wind ___ a'peared. The

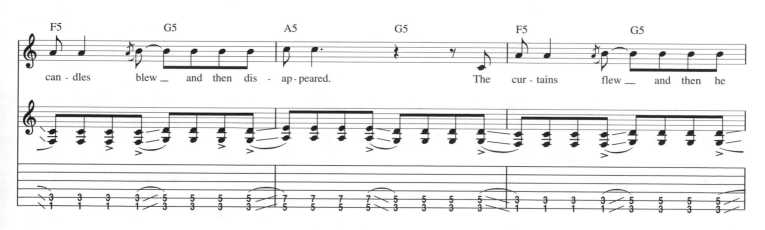

can - dles blew ___ and then dis - ap - peared. The cur - tains flew ___ and then he

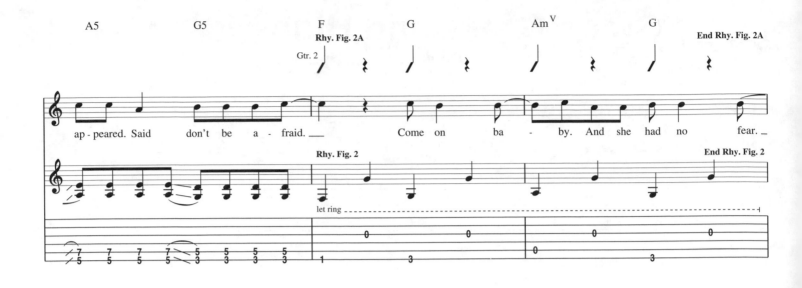

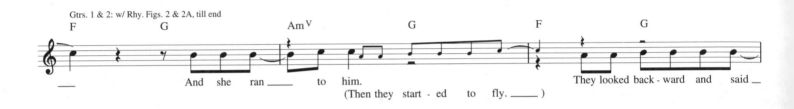

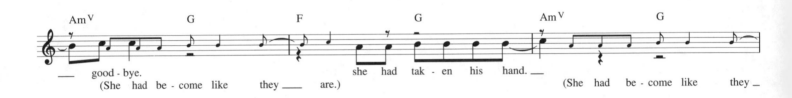

*Two gtrs. arr. for one.

Outro

Play 6 Times and Fade

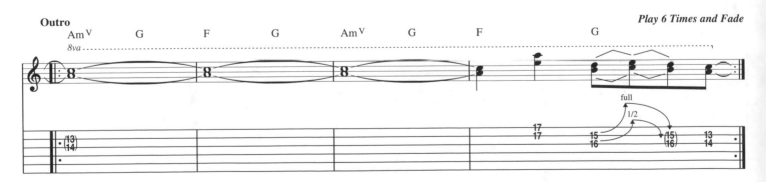

Green Grass and High Tides

Words and Music by Hugh Thomasson Jr.

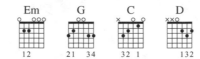

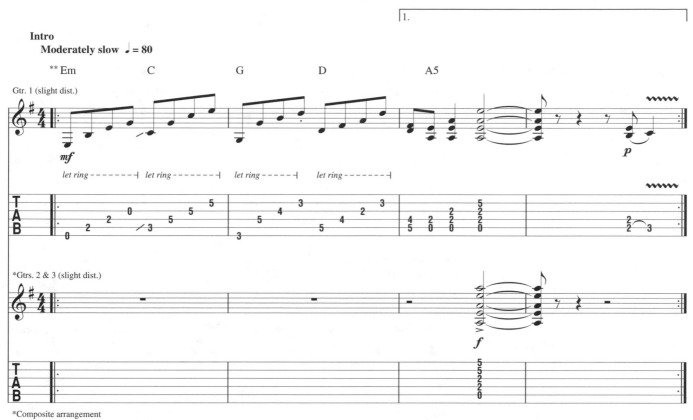

*Composite arrangement

**Chord symbols reflect implied harmony.

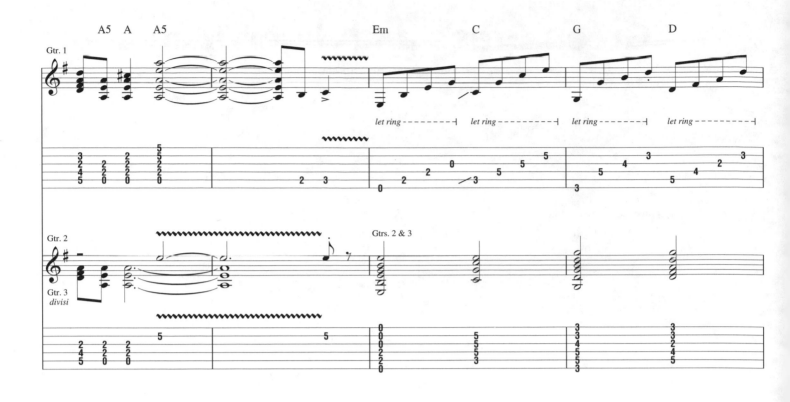

Slightly faster ♩ = 86
Double-time feel

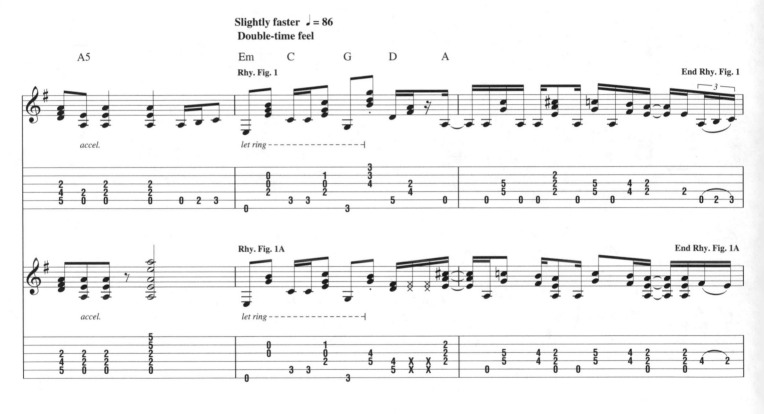

Gtrs. 2 & 3: w/ Rhy. Fig. 1A (3 times)

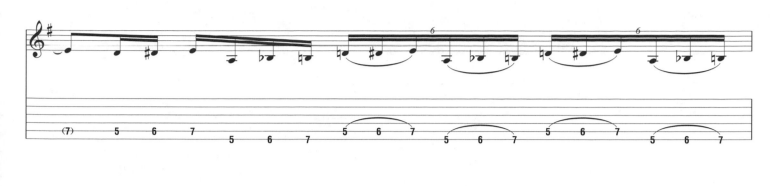

End double-time feel

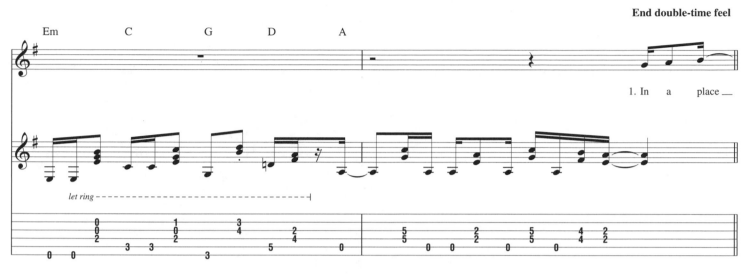

1. In a place ___

Verse

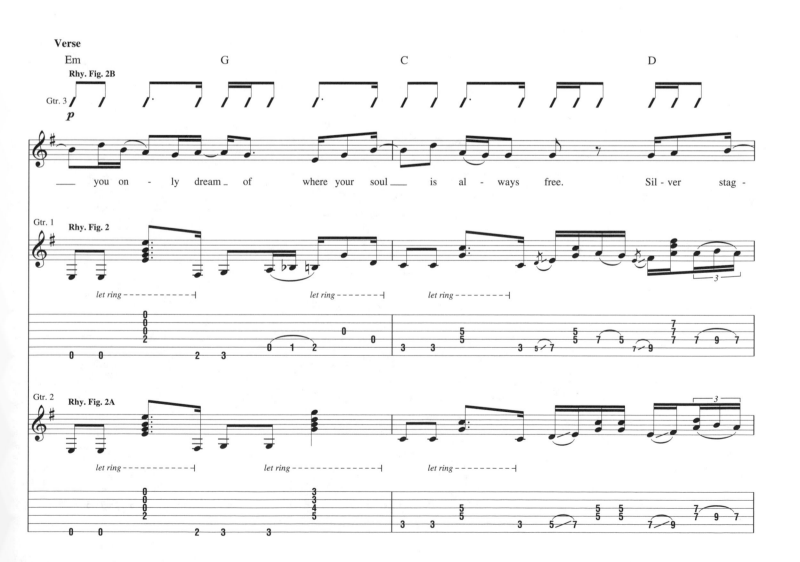

___ you on - ly dream ___ of where your soul ___ is al - ways free. Sil - ver stag -

- es, gold - en cur - tains filled _/_ my head plain as _ could be. _ As a rain-

Gtrs. 1, 2 & 3: w/ Rhy. Figs. 2, 2A & 2B

- bow grew a - round _ the sun, _ all my stars I loved _ who died _ came from some - where be - yond _ the scene. You see, _ these

Gtr. 3: w/ Rhy. Fig. 2B (3 times)

lone - ly peo - ple played _ just for me.

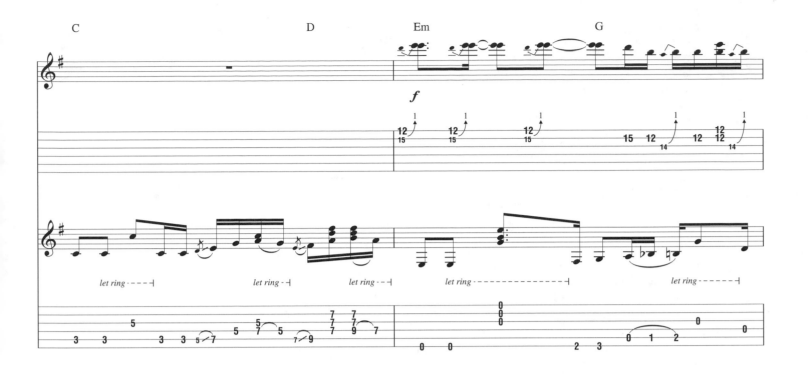

Verse

Gtr. 1: w/ Rhy. Fig. 2 (2 times)

2. Now if I let __ you see this place __ where sto -

Gtr. 2: w/ Rhy. Fig. 2A (last 3 meas.)

- ries all __ ring true. Will you let __ me past __ your face __ to see __ what's real-ly you? __ It's

not for me ___ I ask ___ this quest ___ as though I were a king. ___ For you

have to love, ___ be - lieve, ___ and feel ___ be - fore ___ the burst ___ of tam - bou - rines ___

Chorus

take you there. Green grass and high ___ tides ___ for - ev - ___ er,

*Gtrs. 1 & 2

Rhy. Fig. 3

*Composite arrangement

Cas - tles of stone, ___ stol - en glo - ___ ry. ___ Lost fac - es say ___ we ___ a - dore

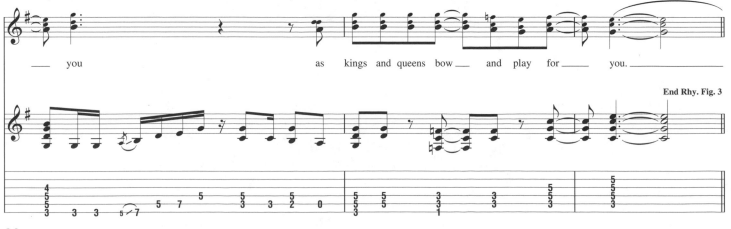

___ you as kings and queens bow ___ and play for ___ you. ___

End Rhy. Fig. 3

Guitar Solo

Gtr. 2: w/ Rhy. Fig. 2A (6 3/4 times)
Gtr. 3: w/ Rhy. Fig. 2B (14 1/4 times)

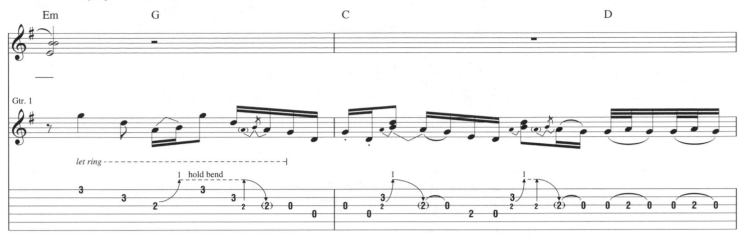

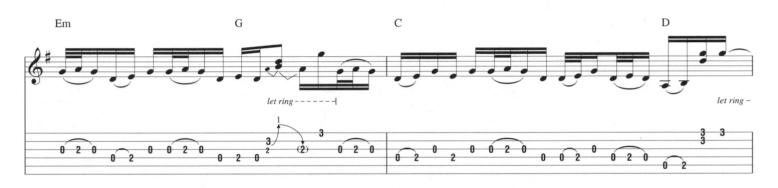

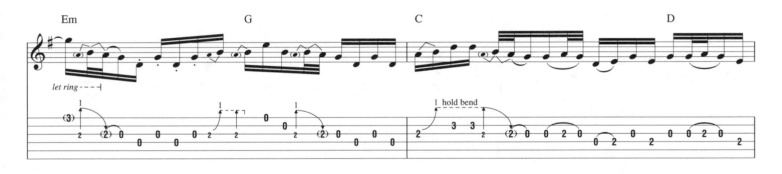

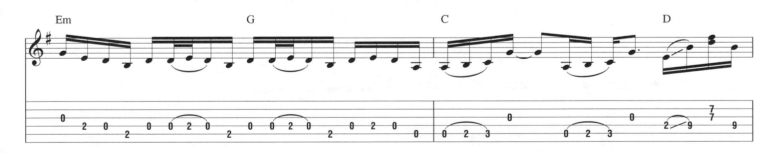

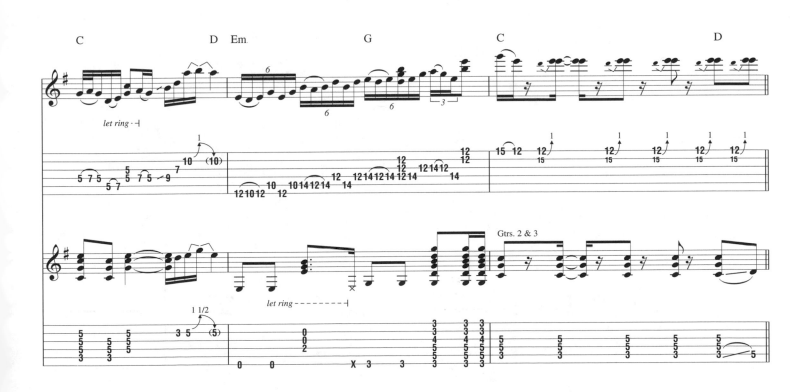

Verse

Gtrs. 1, 2 & 3: w/ Rhy. Figs. 2, 2A & 2B (2 times)

3. Those who don't _ be - lieve _ me find _ your souls _ and set _ them free. _ Those who do, _ be - lieve _ and love _ as time _

_ will be your key. _ Time and time _ a - gain _ I've thanked _ them for _ a peace _ of mind. _ They

Gtrs. 1 & 2: w/ Rhy. Fills 1 & 1A

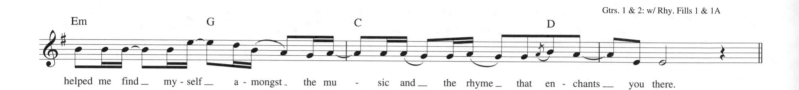

helped me find _ my - self _ a - mongst _ the mu - sic and _ the rhyme _ that en - chants _ you there.

Chorus

Gtrs. 1 & 2: w/ Rhy. Fig. 3

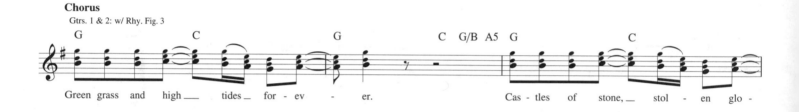

Green grass and high _ tides _ for - ev - er. Cas - tles of stone, _ stol - en glo -

- ry. _ Lost fac - es say _ we a - dore _ you as kings and queens bow _ and play for _

Outro - Guitar Solo
Double-time feel

Gtr. 1: w/ Rhy. Fig. 1 (2 times)
Gtr. 2: w/ Rhy. Fig. 1A (22 times)

_ you. _ Yeah, they play just for _ you. _

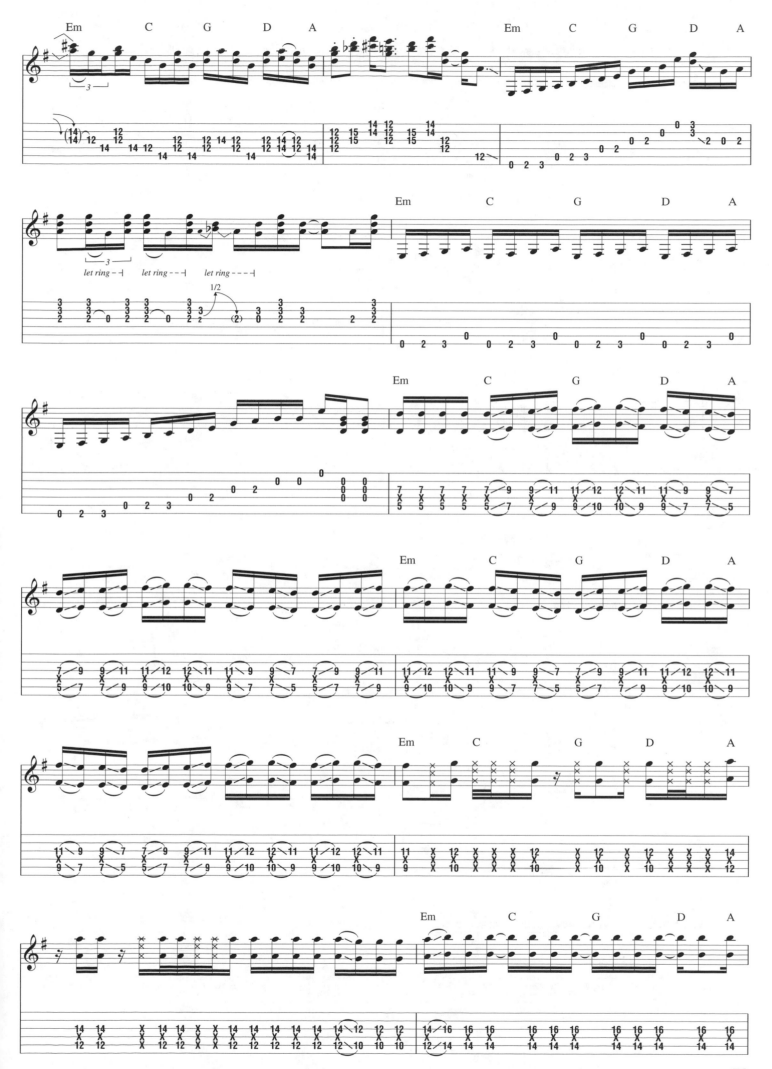

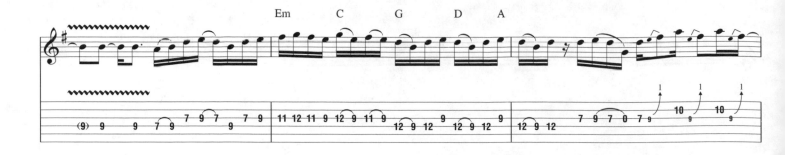

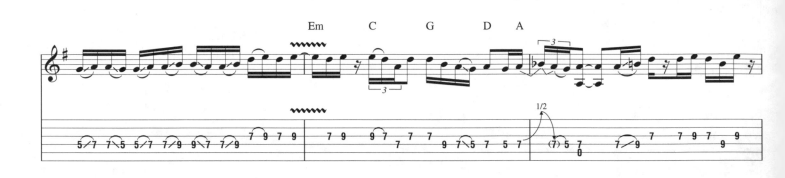

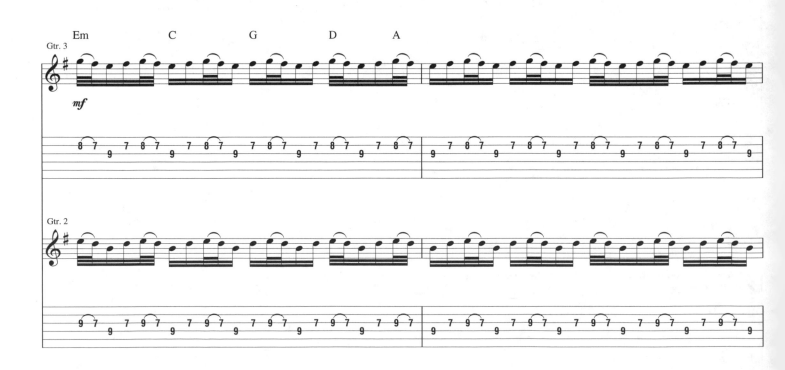

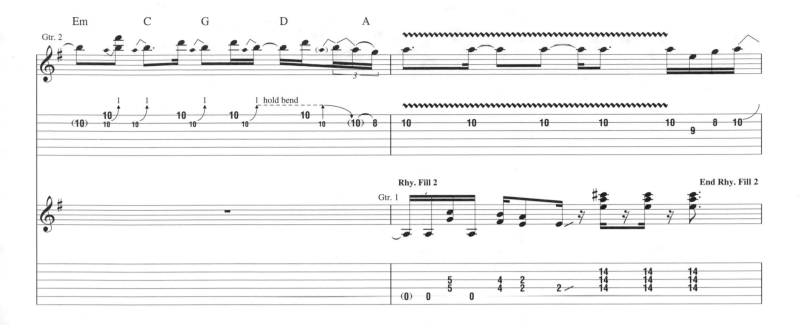

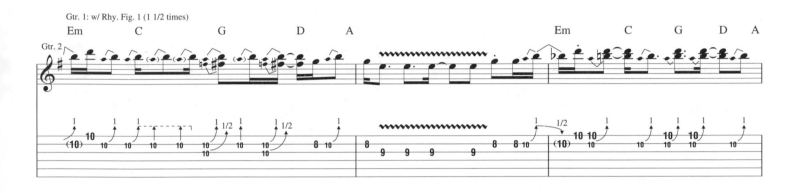

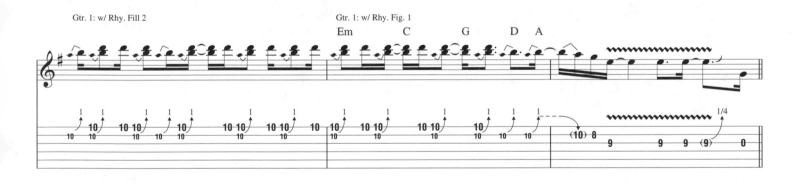

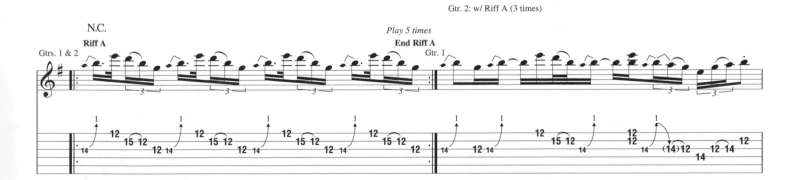

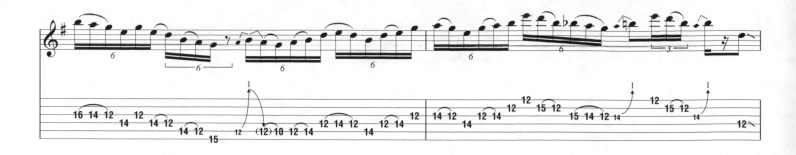

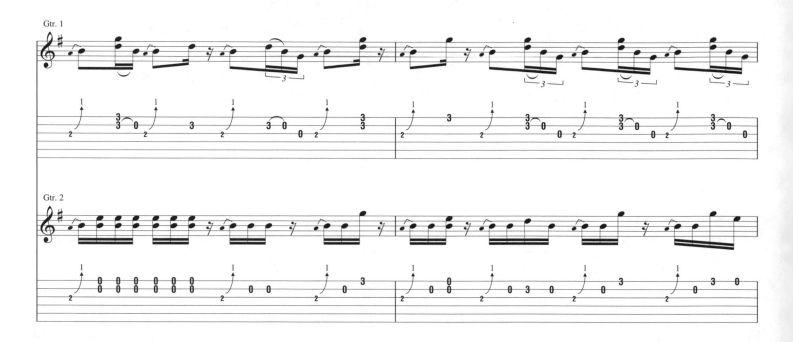

Gtr. 1

Gtr. 2

Gtrs. 1 & 2: w/ Riff A (4 times)

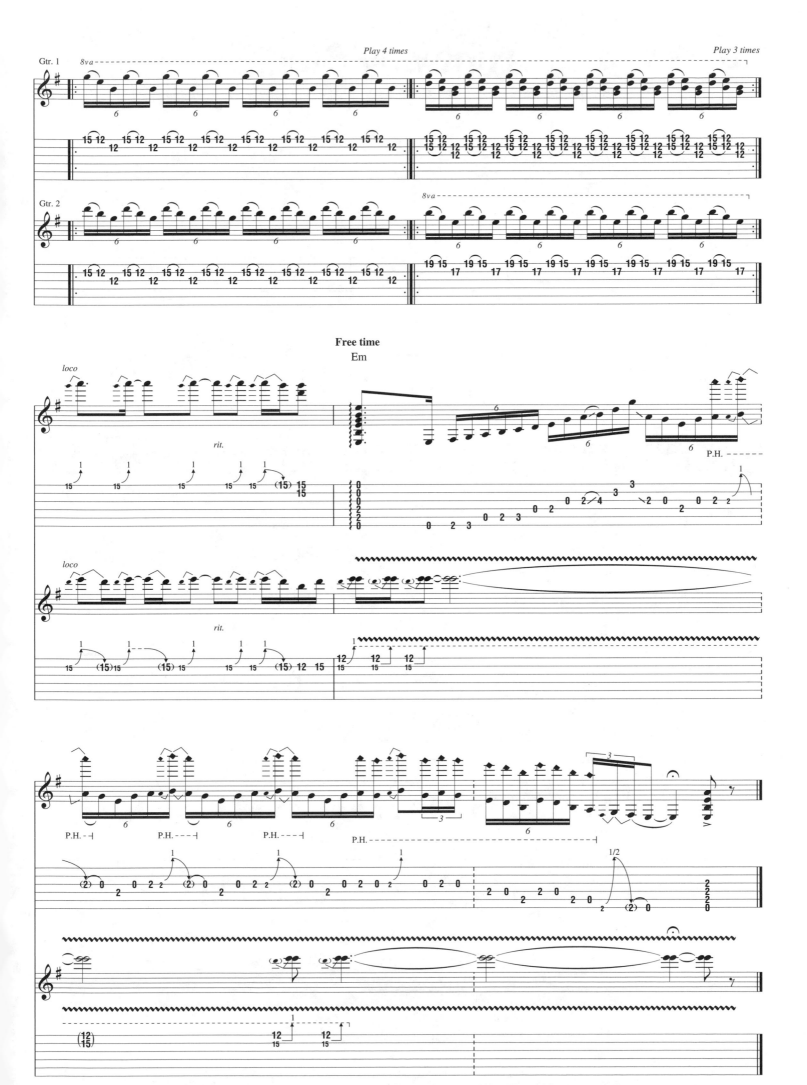

Highway Star

Words and Music by Ritchie Blackmore, Ian Gillan, Roger Glover, Jon Lord and Ian Paice

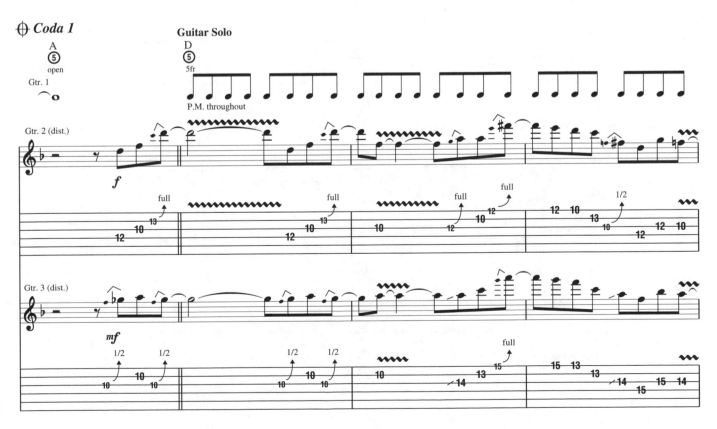

Gtr. 1: w/ Rhy. Fig. 3, 2nd time, simile

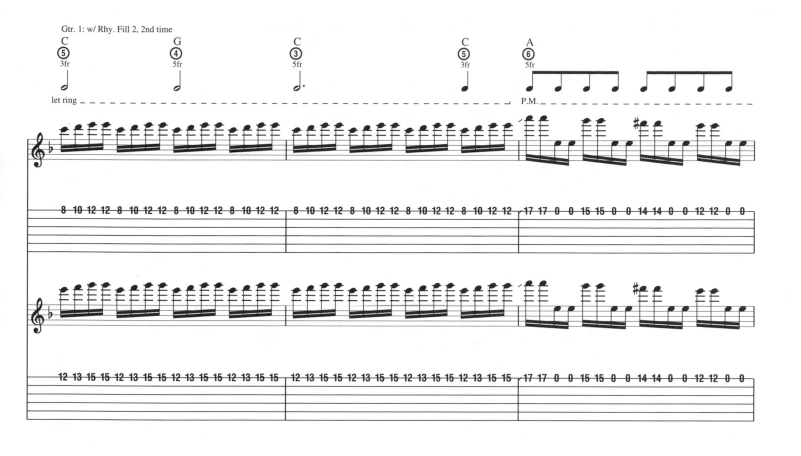

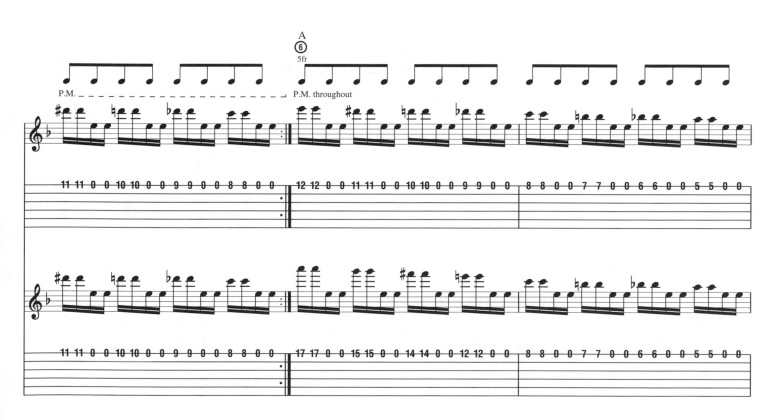

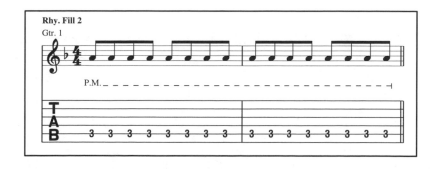

D.S. al Coda 2
(1st lyrics)
Gtr. 1: w/ Rhy. Fill 1

90

I'm So Sick

Words and Music by Sameer Bhattacharya, Jared Hartmann, Kirkpatrick Seals, James Culpepper and Lacey Mosley

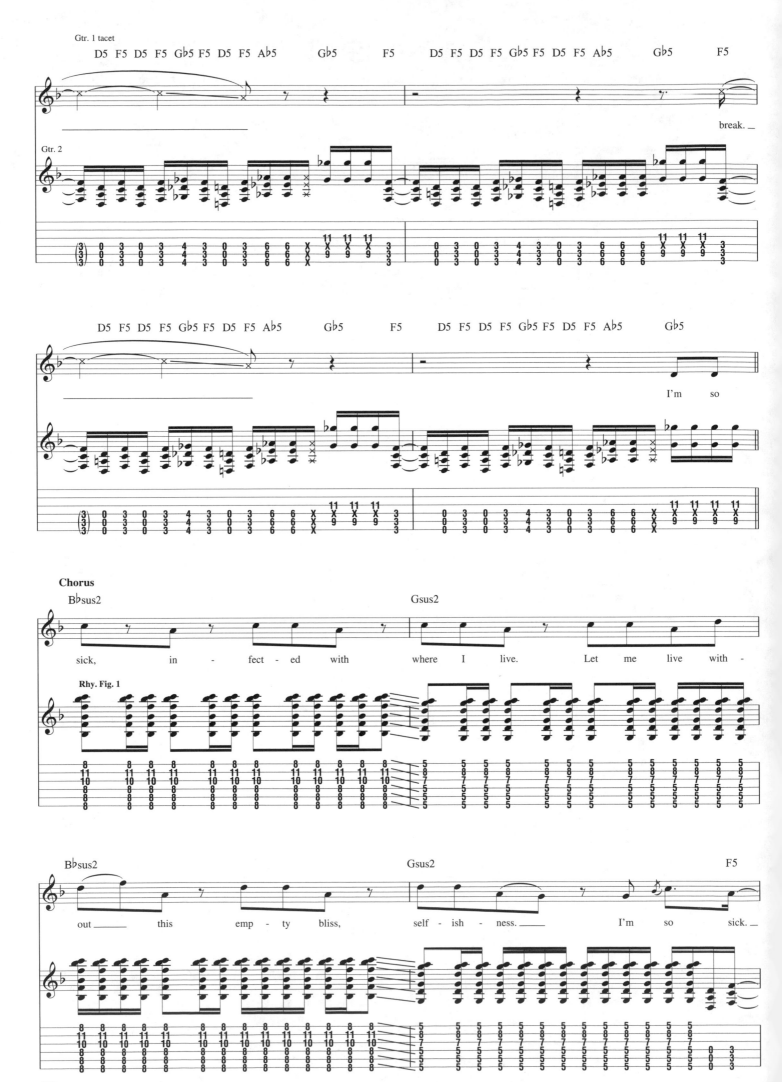

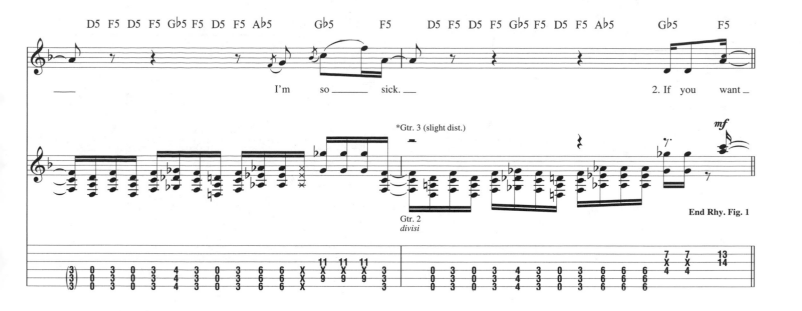

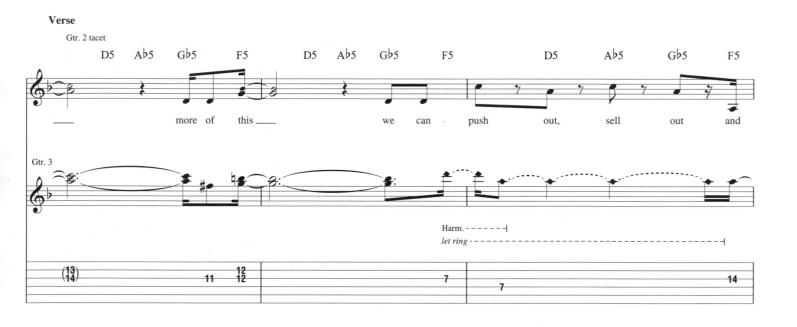

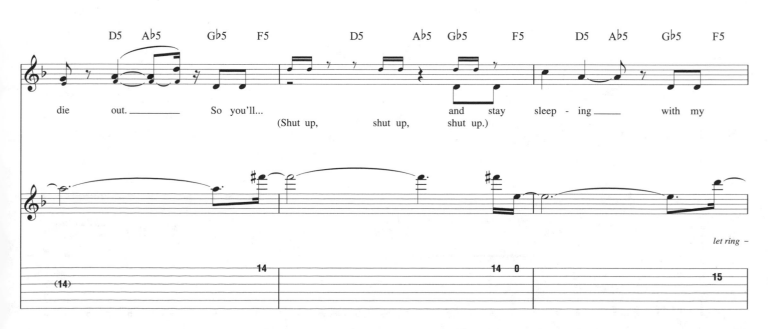

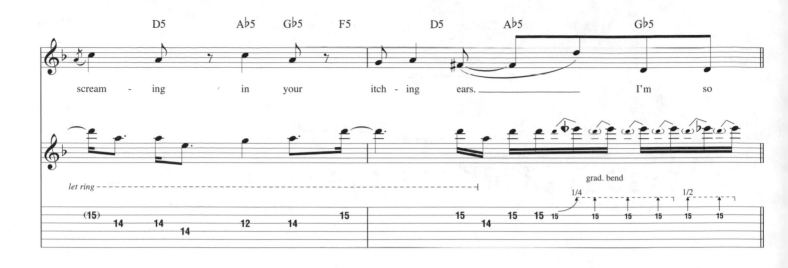

scream - ing in your itch - ing ears. _____ I'm so

Chorus

Gtr. 2: w/ Rhy. Fig. 1
Gtr. 3 tacet

sick, in - fect - ed with where I live. Let me live with - out _ this emp - ty bliss, self - ish - ness. _ I'm so sick.

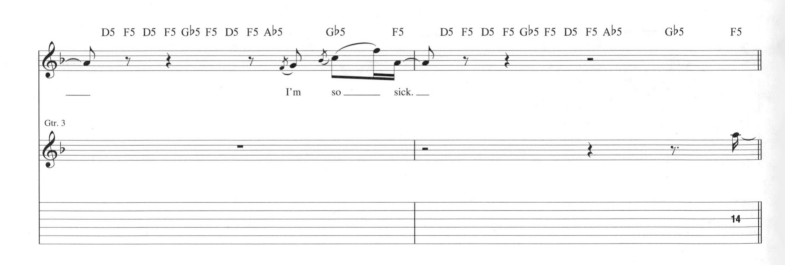

I'm so _____ sick. _

Gtr. 3

Verse

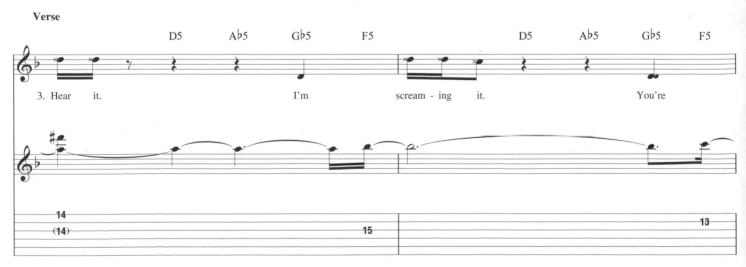

3. Hear it. I'm scream - ing it. You're

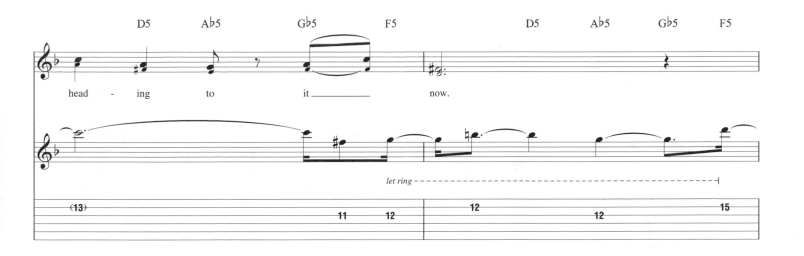

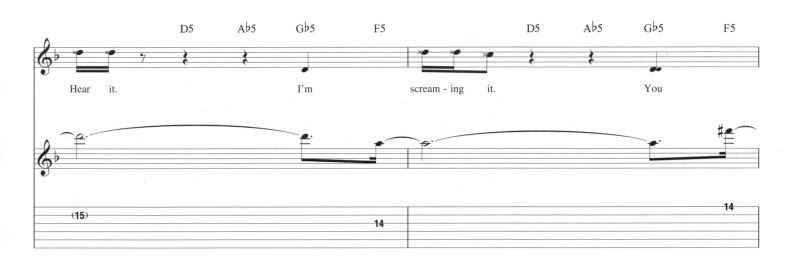

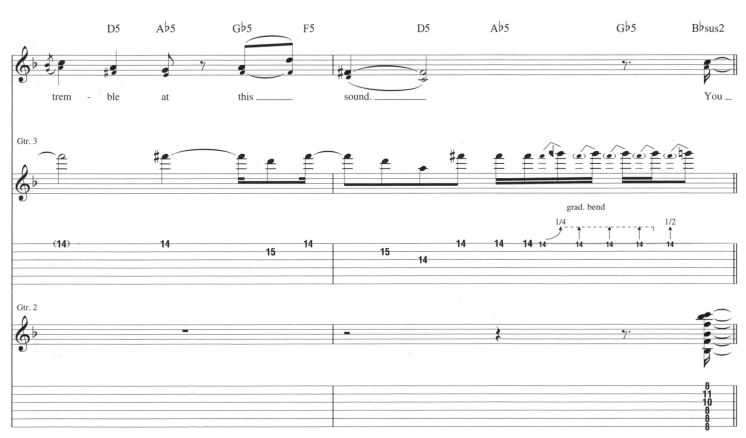

Bridge

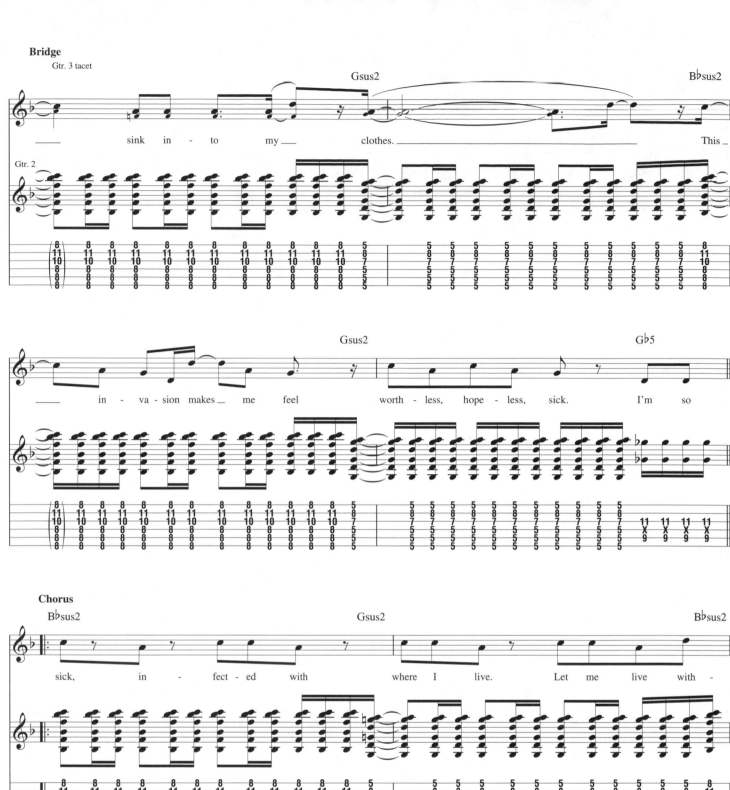

Chorus

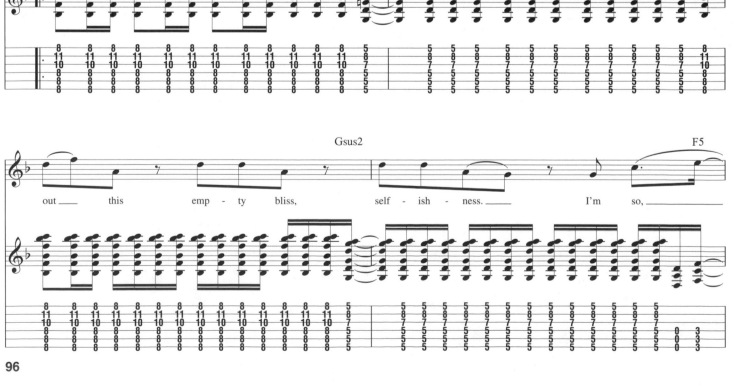

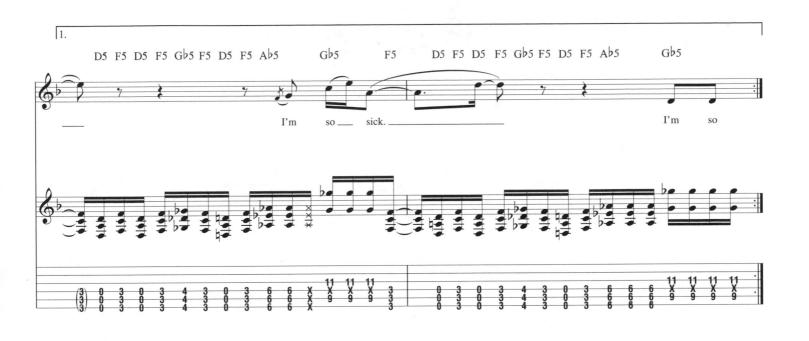

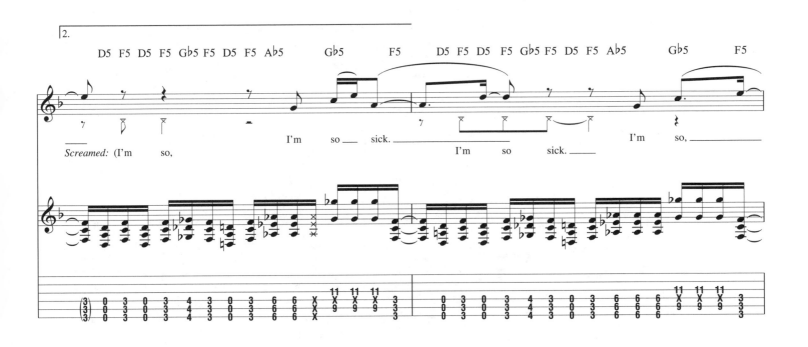

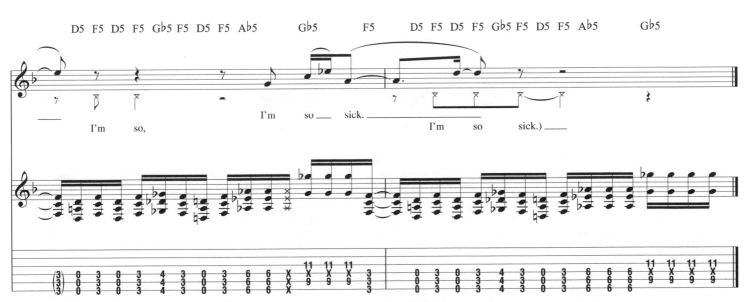

In Bloom

Words and Music by Kurt Cobain

Intro
Moderately slow Rock ♩ = 78

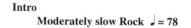
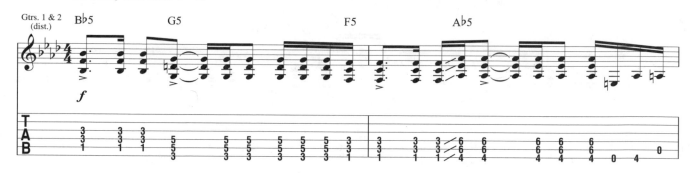
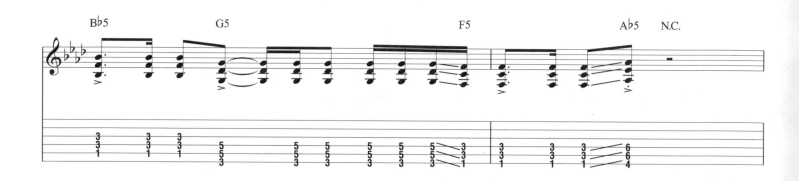
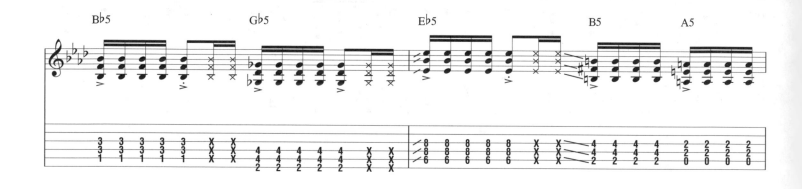
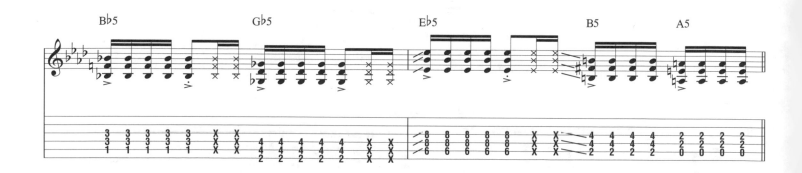

Verse

Gtrs. 1 & 2 tacet

1. Sell   the kids   for food. _____
2. We   can have   some more. _____

*Gtr. 3

*Bass arr. for gtr.

Weath - er chang - es moods. _____
Na - ture is _____ a whore. _____

Gtr. 3 tacet

| Bb | Gb | Eb | B | A |

Spring   is here _____ a - gain. _____
Bruis - es on _____ the fruit. _____

Gtr. 1

mf

w/ clean tone

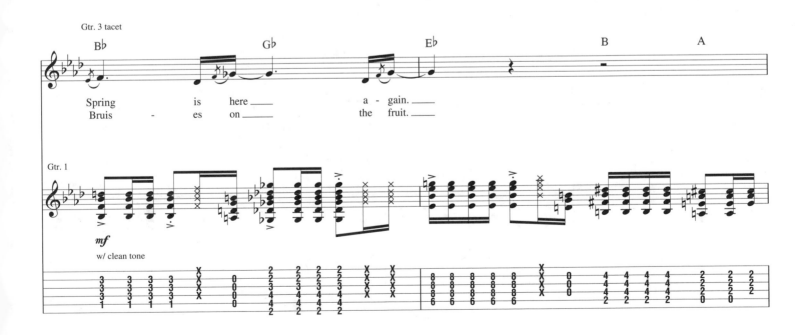

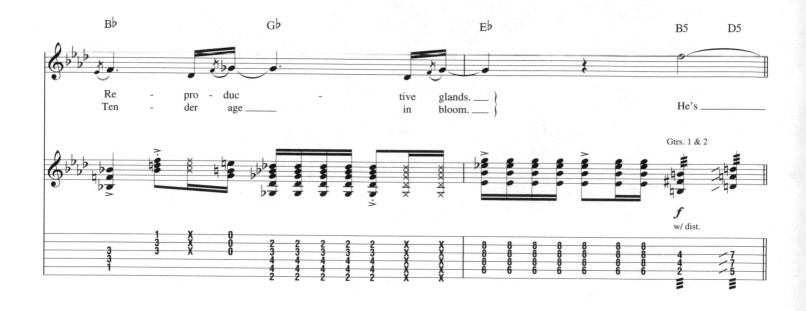

Re - pro - duc - tive glands. ___ }
Ten - der age ___ in bloom. ___ }

He's ___

𝄋 Chorus

___ the one ___ who likes all our pret - ty songs ___ and he

Rhy. Fig. 1

likes to sing a - long ___ and he likes to shoot his gun, ___ but he

End Rhy. Fig. 1

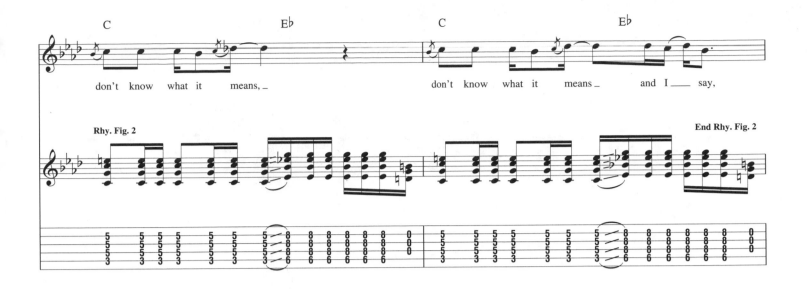

don't know what it means, ___   don't know what it means ___ and I ___ say,

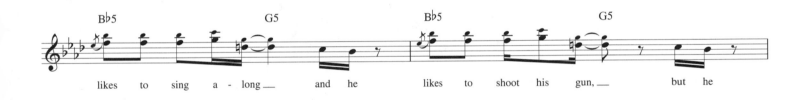

he's   the one ___ who likes   all our pret - ty songs ___ and he

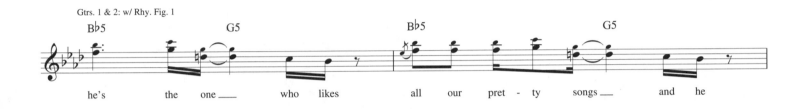

likes to sing a - long ___ and he   likes to shoot his gun, ___ but he

To Coda ⊕

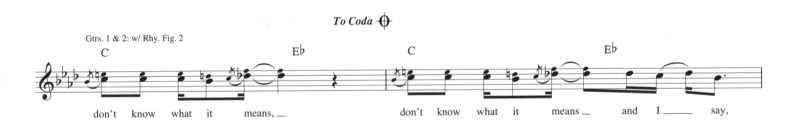

don't know what it means, ___   don't know what it means ___ and I ___ say,

"Yeah." ___   Mm.

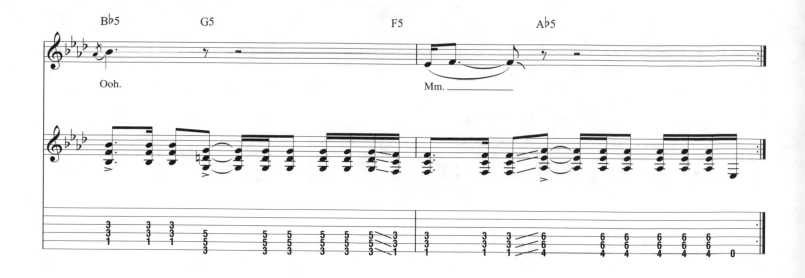

Guitar Solo

Gtr. 2 tacet

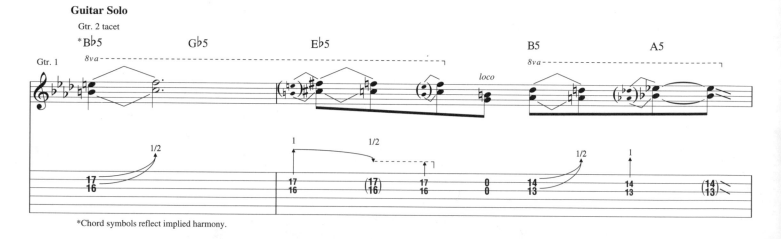

*Chord symbols reflect implied harmony.

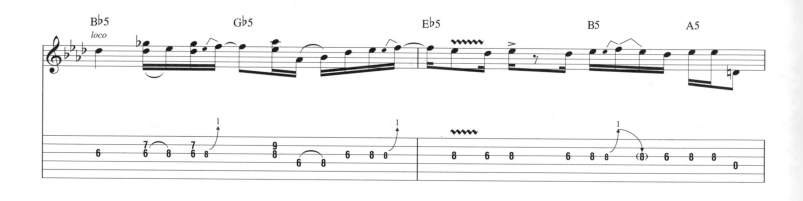

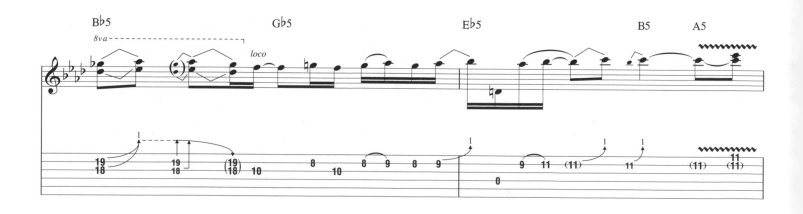

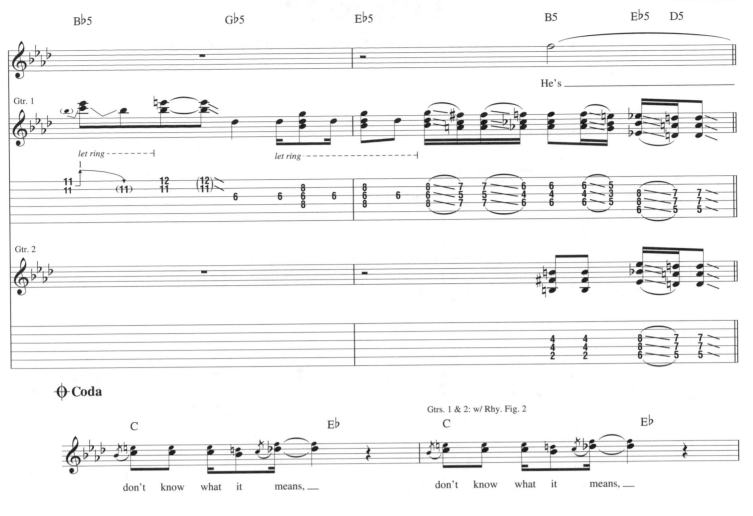

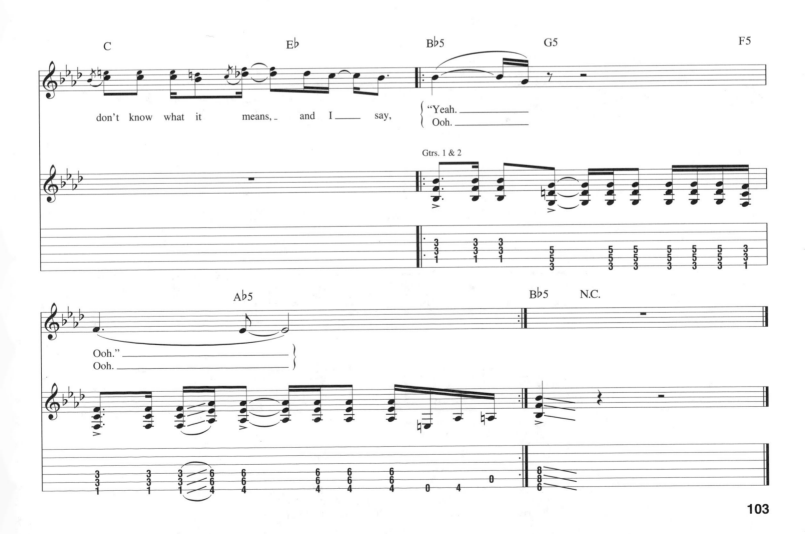

Learn to Fly

Words and Music by Dave Grohl, Nate Mendel and Taylor Hawkins

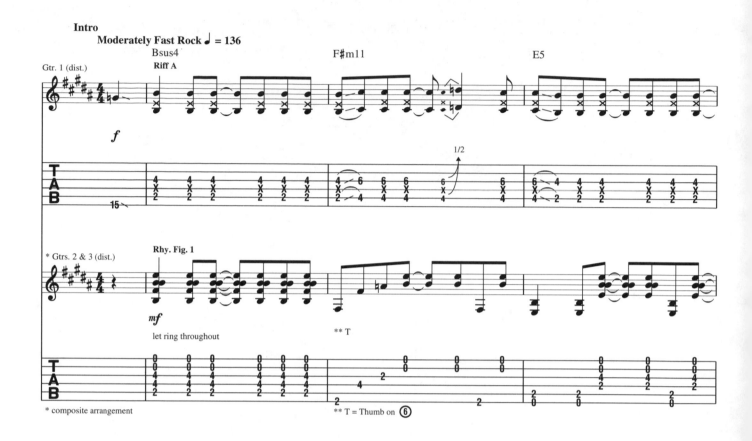

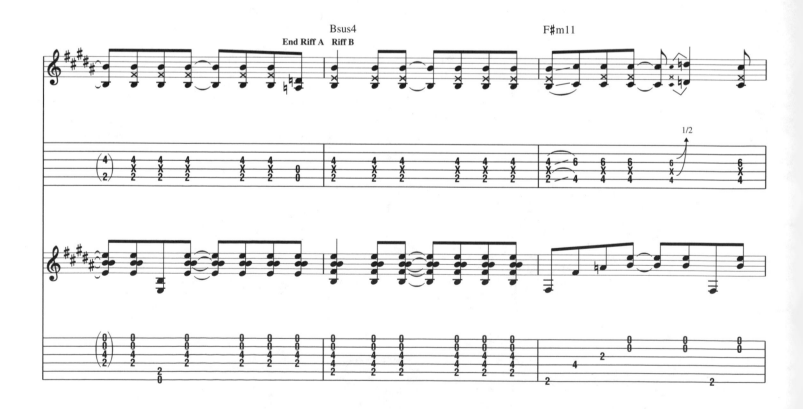

Hook me up a new rev-o-lu-tion, 'cause this one is ___ a lie. ___

___ I sat a-round laugh-ing and watched ___ the last ___ one die.

* w/ echo repeats

𝄋 Chorus

Gtr. 1: w/ Riff A, 3rd time

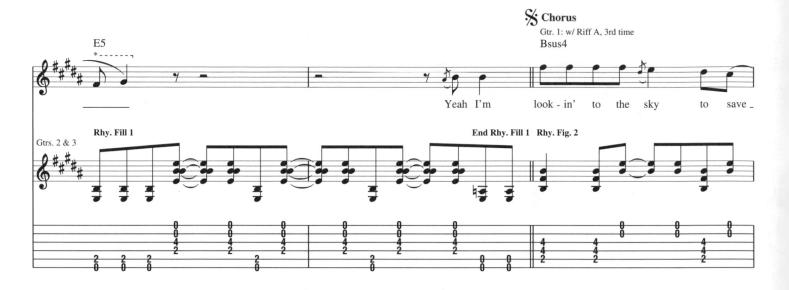

___ Yeah I'm look-in' to the sky to save ___

Gtrs. 2 & 3

Rhy. Fill 1   End Rhy. Fill 1   Rhy. Fig. 2

Gtr. 4: w/ Fill 2, 2nd & 3rd times, simile

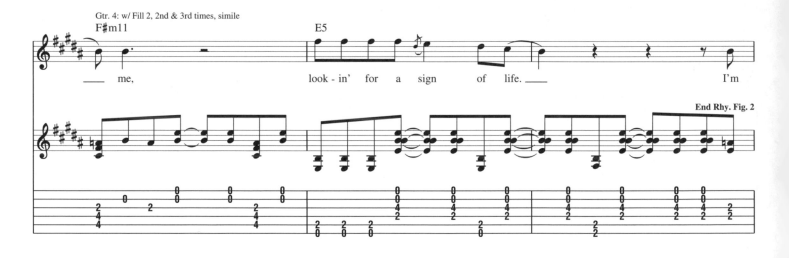

___ me,   look-in' for a sign of life. ___   I'm

End Rhy. Fig. 2

Gtrs. 2 & 3: w/ Rhy. Fig. 2, 1 3/4 times, simile
Gtr. 1: w/ Riff B, 3rd time
Gtr. 4: w/ Fill 2, 2nd & 3rd times, simile

look-in' for some-thin' to help ___ me burn ___ out bright. ___   I'm

Gtr. 1: w/ Riff A, 1st 3 meas., 3rd time
Gtr. 4: w/ Fill 2, 2nd & 3rd times, simile

look-in' for a comp-li-ca-tion,   look-in' 'cause I'm tired of { ly- / try-

Verse

Gtr. 1: w/ Fill 1
Gtr. 2: w/ Riff C, 3 1/2 times, simile
Gtr. 4 tacet

think I'm dy - in' mis-sing pa - tience, it can wait __ one night. __

Riff D

End Riff D

* Chord symbols reflect combined tonality.

Gtr. 3: w/ Riff D, 2 1/2 times

Badd9   F#m11   Esus2

Give it all a - way if you give __ me one __ last try. __

* w/ echo repeats

Badd9   F#m11

We'll live hap - pi - ly ev - er trapped __ if you __

Esus2   Badd9

__ just save __ my life. __ Run - nin' down the an - gels and ev -

D.S. al Coda 1

F#m11   Gtrs. 2 & 3: w/ Rhy. Fill 1, simile   E5

- 'ry - thing's __ all __ right. __ I'm

⊕ Coda 1

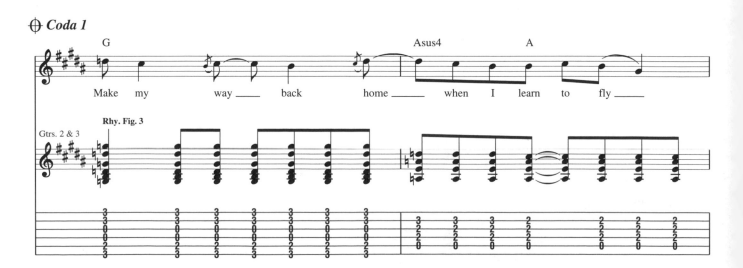

G   Asus4   A

Make my way __ back home __ when I learn to fly __

Rhy. Fig. 3

Gtrs. 2 & 3

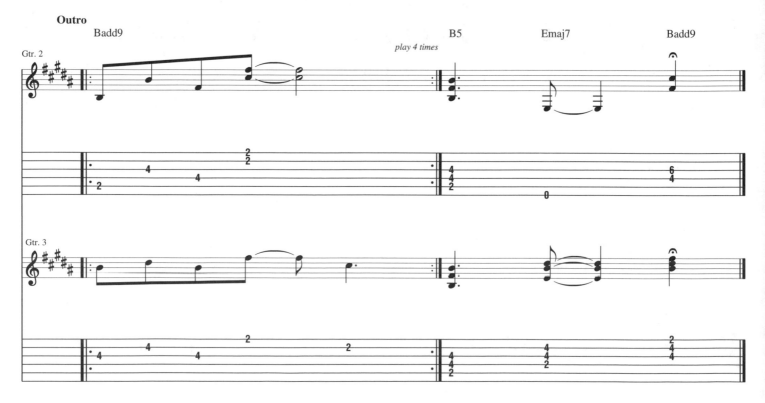

Long Time

Words and Music by Tom Scholz

Intro
Moderately ♩ = 118

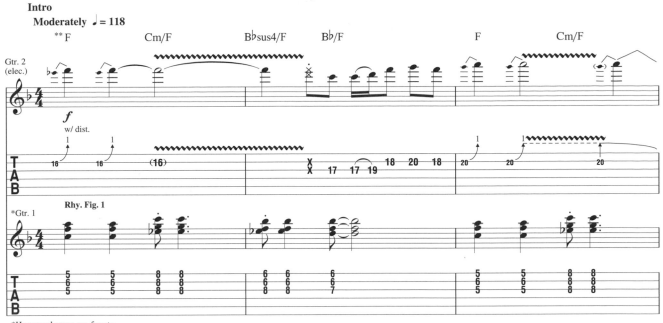

*Hammond organ arr. for gtr.
**Chord symbols reflect overall harmony.

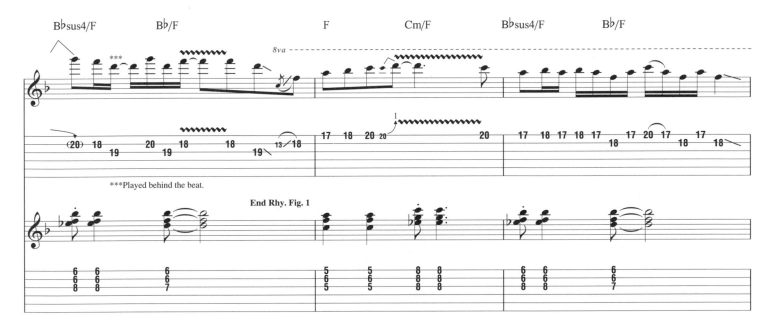

***Played behind the beat.

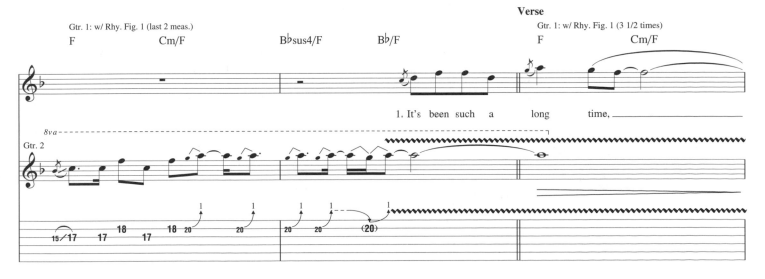

1. It's been such a long time,

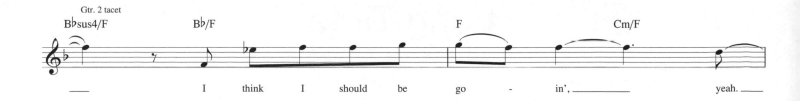

I think I should be go - in', _____ yeah. ____

And time does - n't wait for me, _____

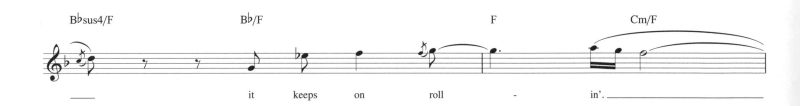

it keeps on roll - in'. _____

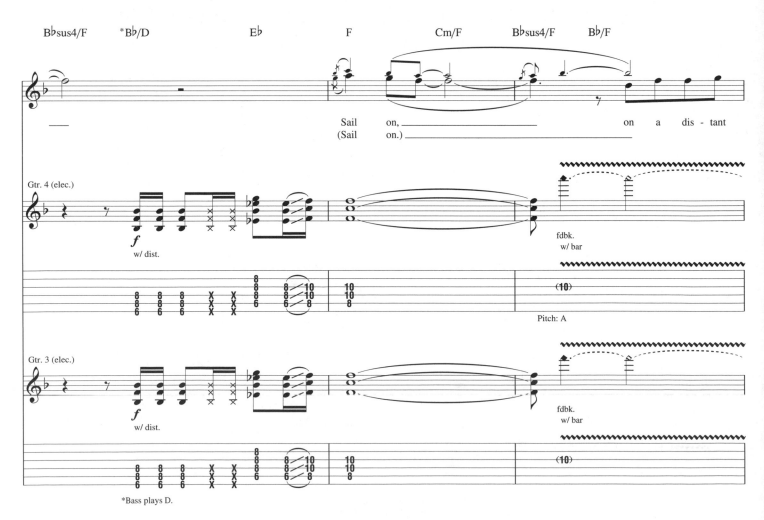

Sail on, _____ on a dis - tant
(Sail on.) _____

Gtr. 4 (elec.)

f
w/ dist.

fdbk.
w/ bar

Pitch: A

Gtr. 3 (elec.)

f
w/ dist.

fdbk.
w/ bar

*Bass plays D.

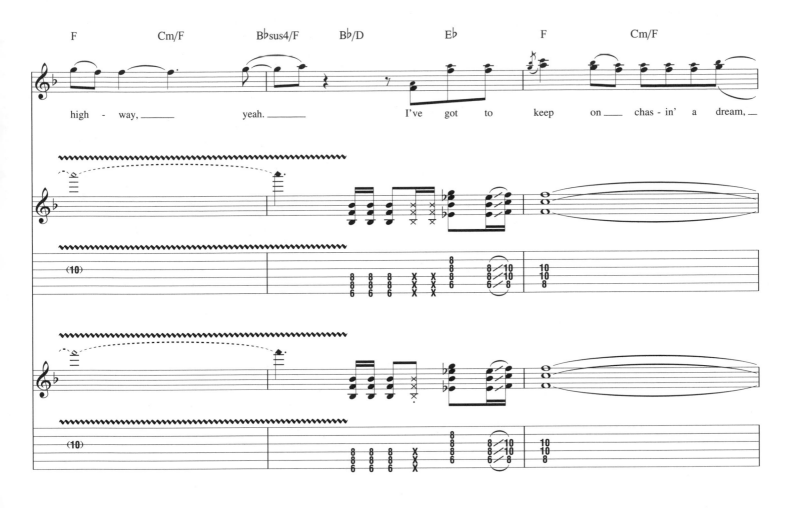

high-way, _____ yeah. _____ I've got to keep on _____ chas-in' a dream, _____

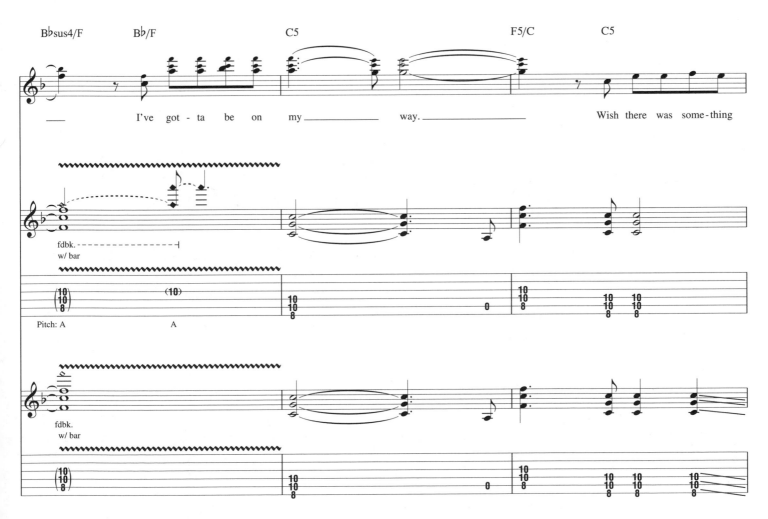

_____ I've got-ta be on my _____ way. _____ Wish there was some-thing

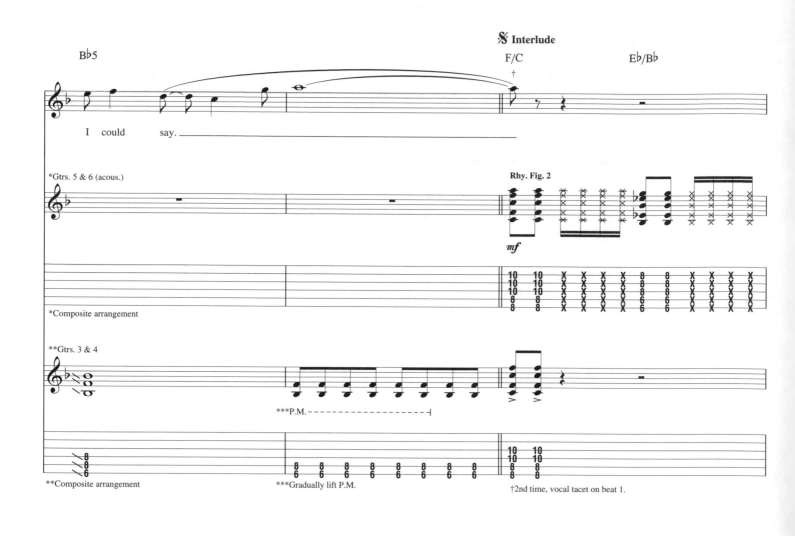

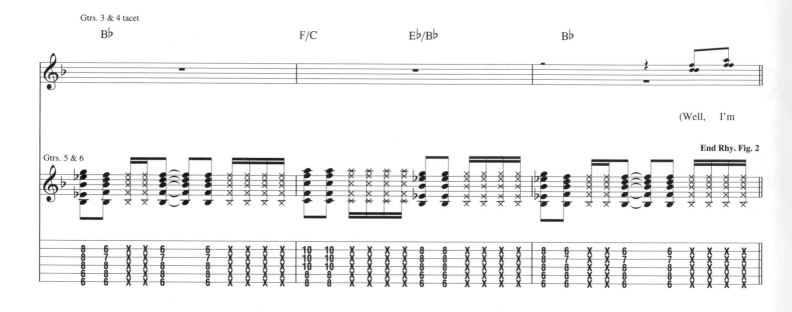

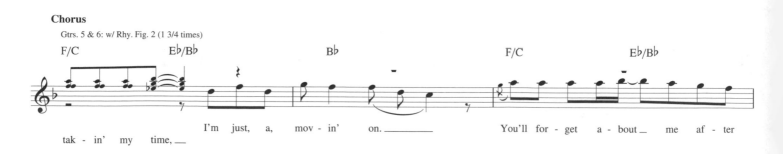

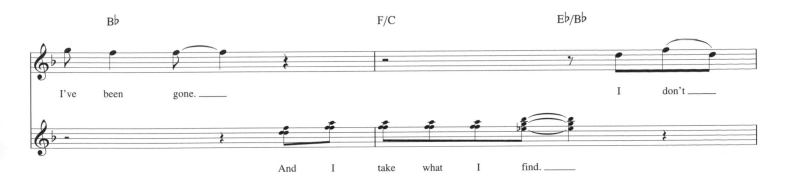

I've been gone. ___

And I take what I find.

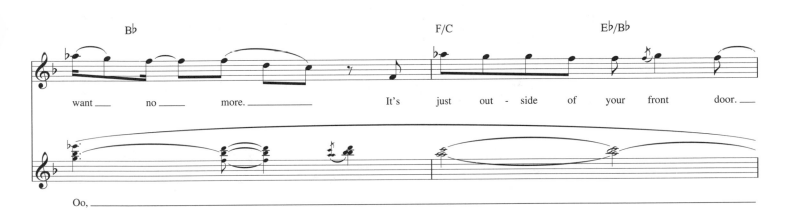

want ___ no ___ more. ___ It's just out-side of your front door. ___

Oo, ___

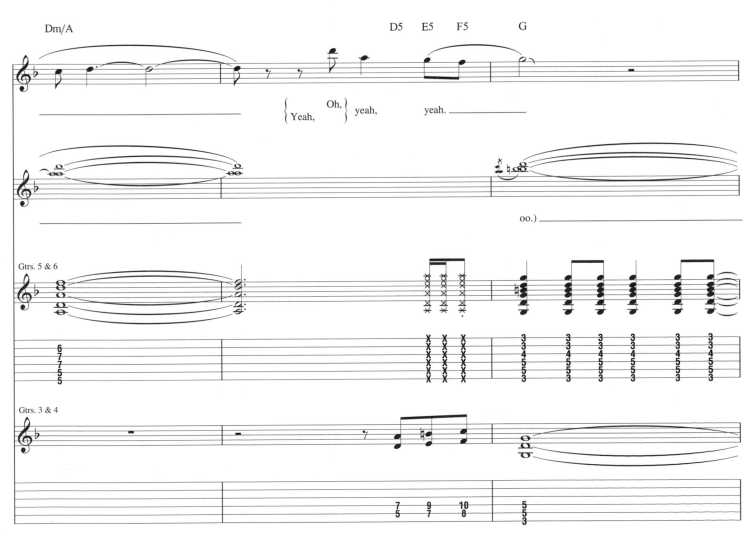

{ Yeah, Oh, } yeah, yeah. ___

oo.) ___

Gtrs. 5 & 6

Gtrs. 3 & 4

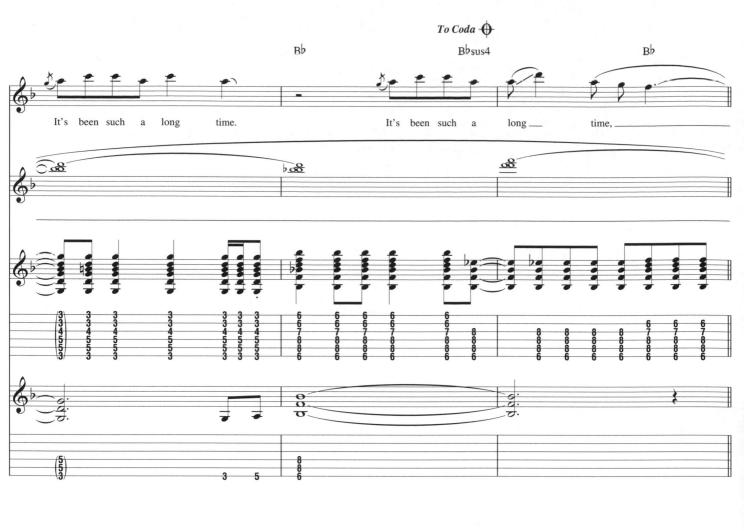

It's been such a long time. It's been such a long ___ time, ___

Guitar Solo

Gtr. 1: w/ Rhy. Fig. 1 (2 times)
Gtrs. 5 & 6 tacet

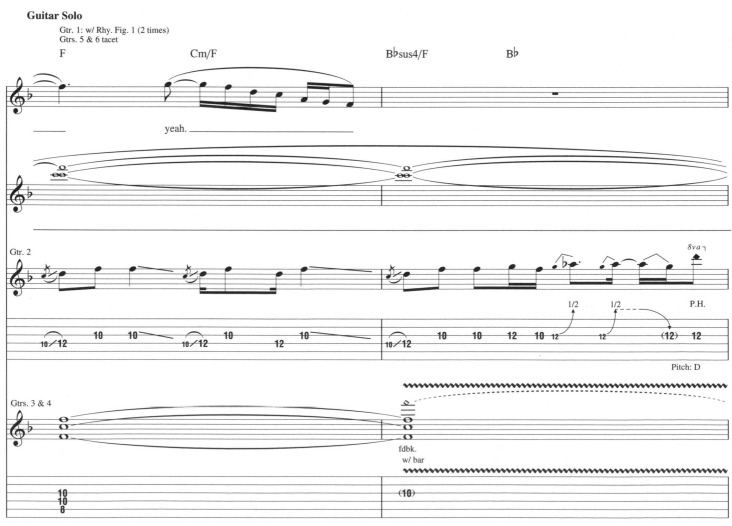

___ yeah. ___

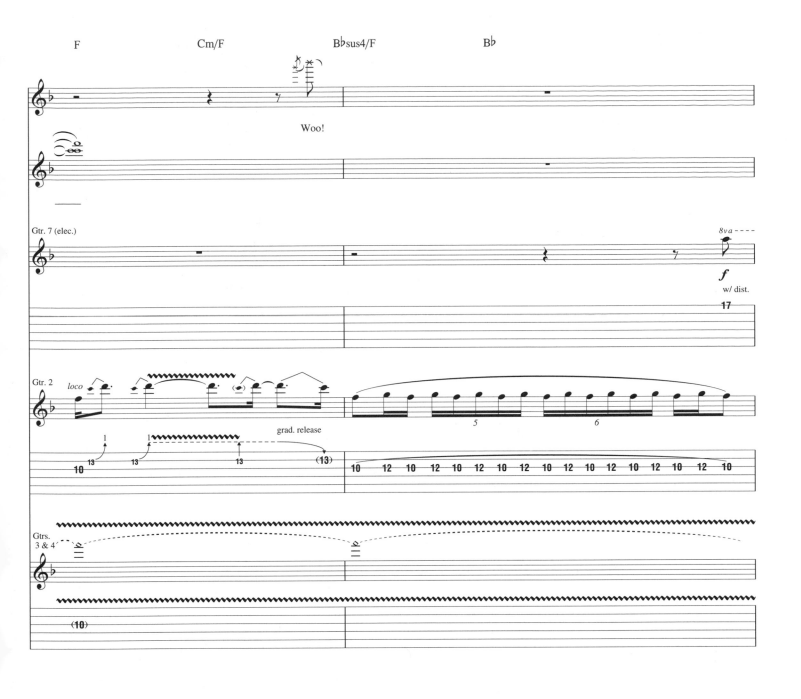

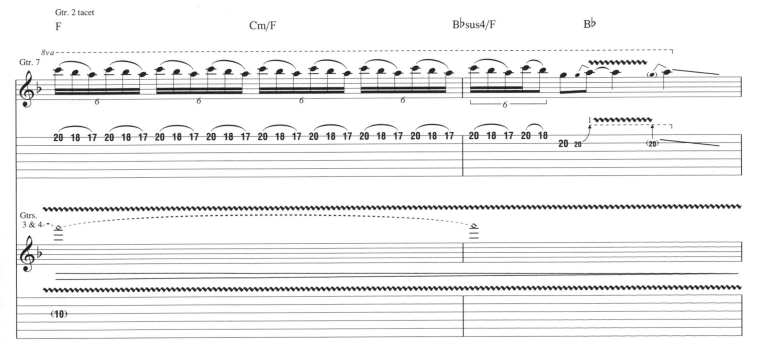

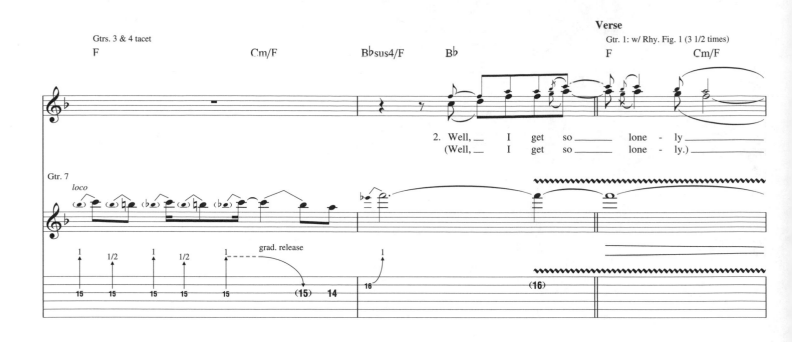

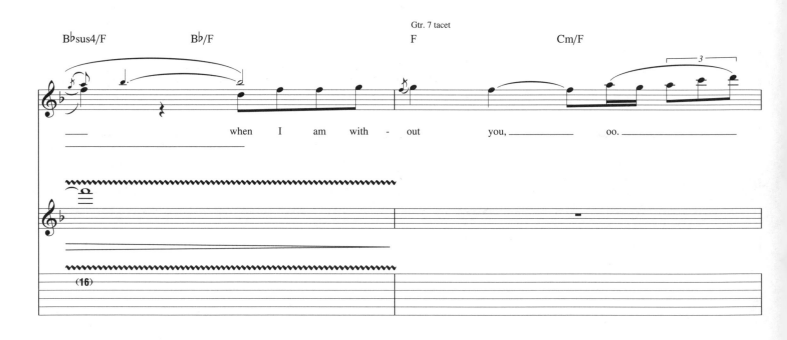

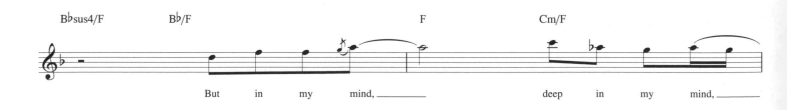

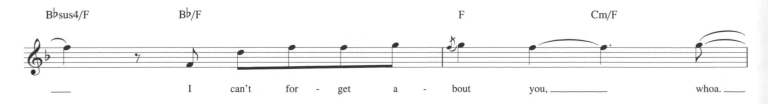

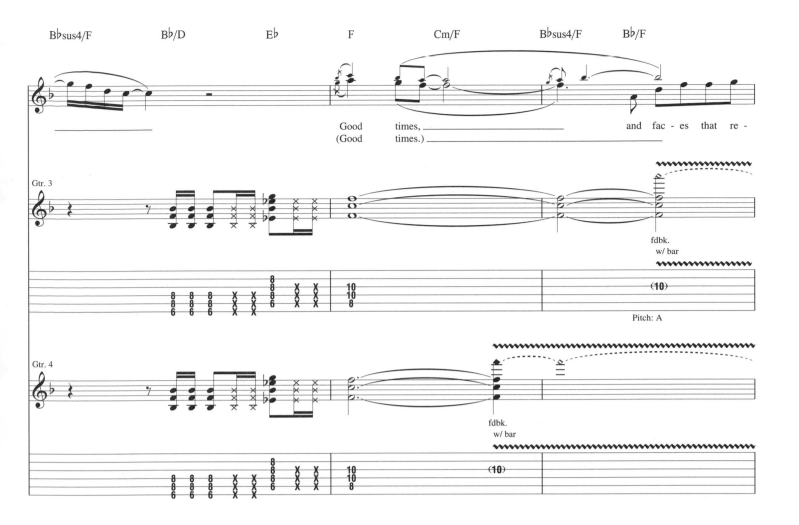

Good times, _____ and fac - es that re -
(Good times.) _____

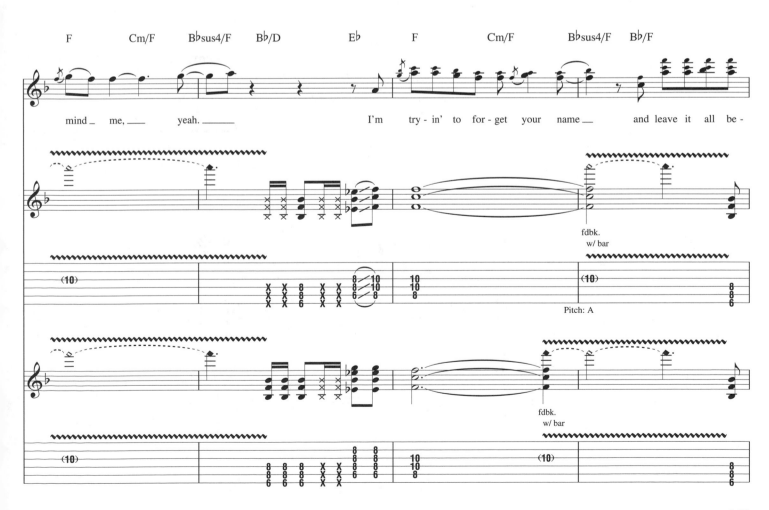

mind_ me, _ yeah. _____ I'm try - in' to for - get your name _ and leave it all be -

119

hind _____ me. You're com - in' back to find ___ me. _____

⊕ Coda

Interlude

long   time. _____

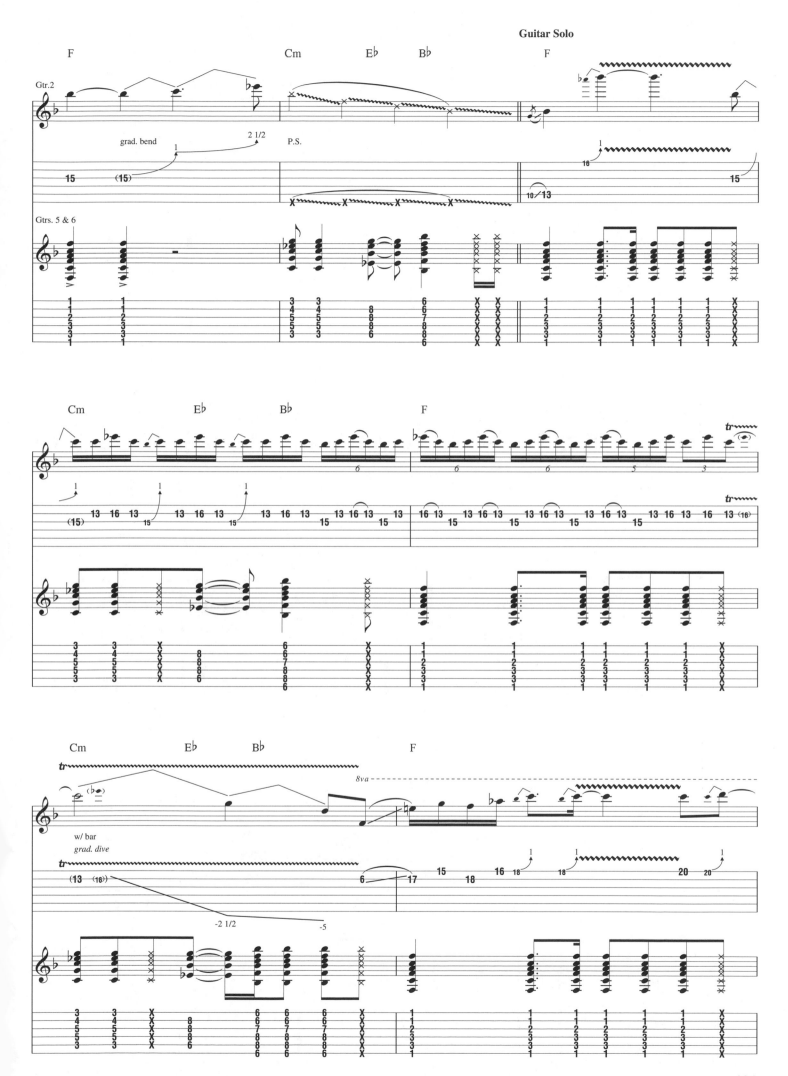

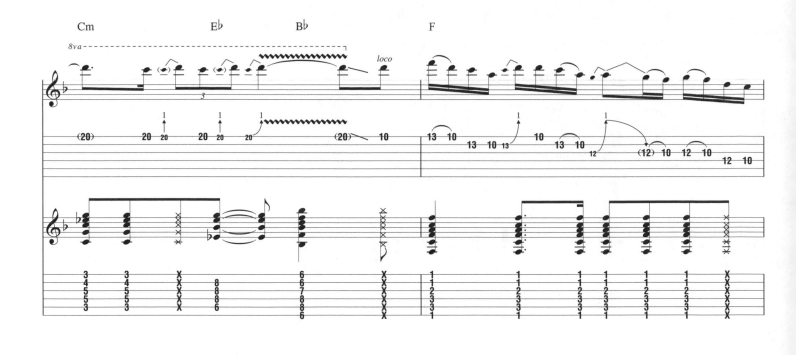

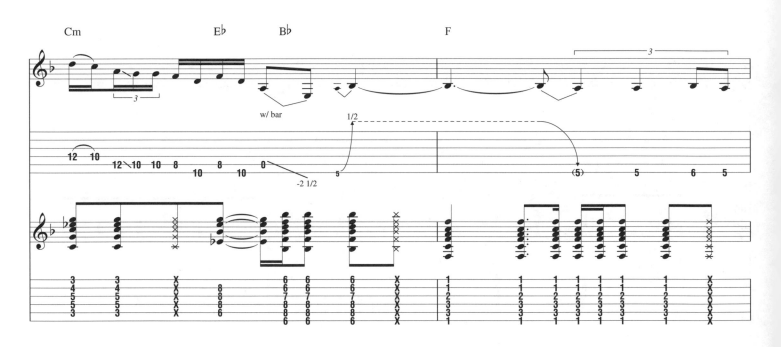

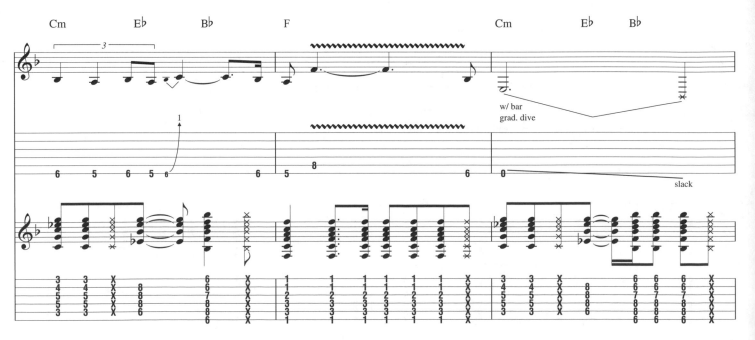

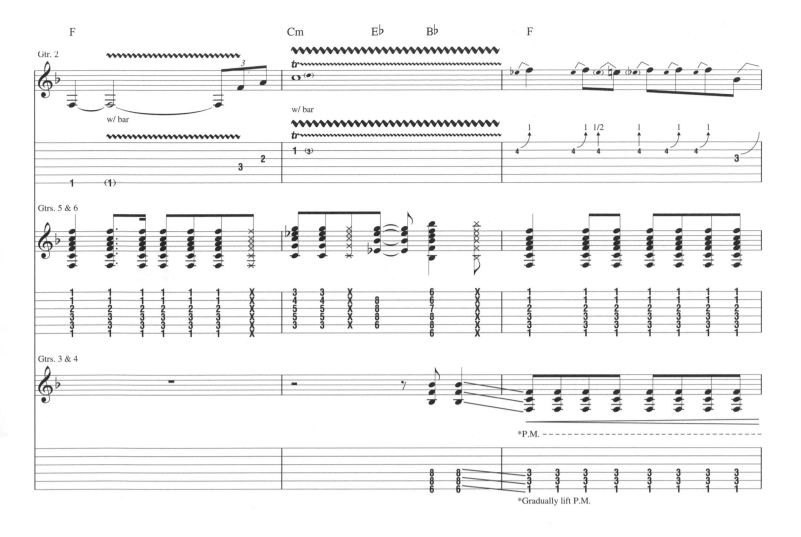

Interlude

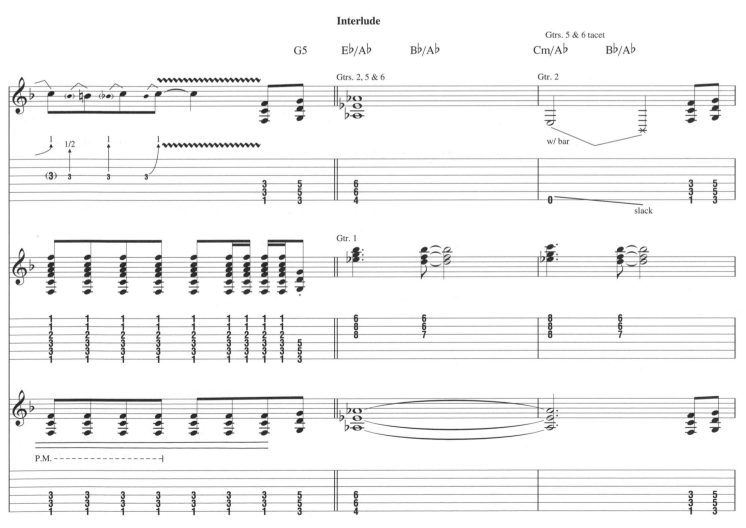

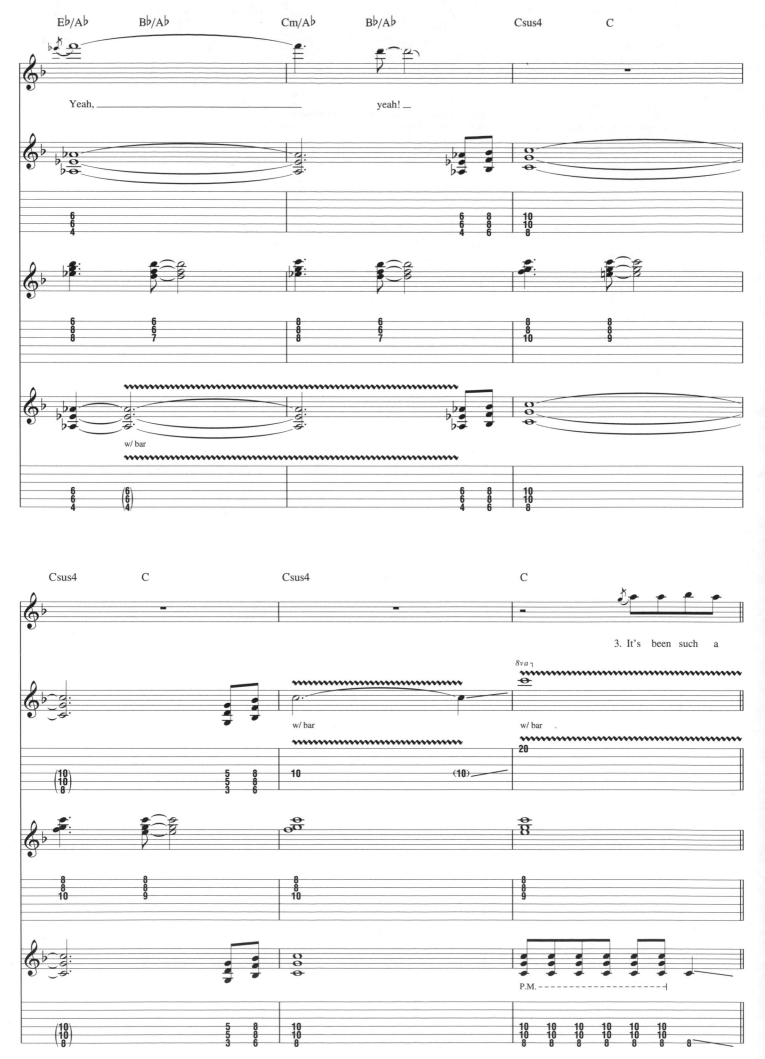

Yeah, _____ yeah! __

3. It's been such a

Verse

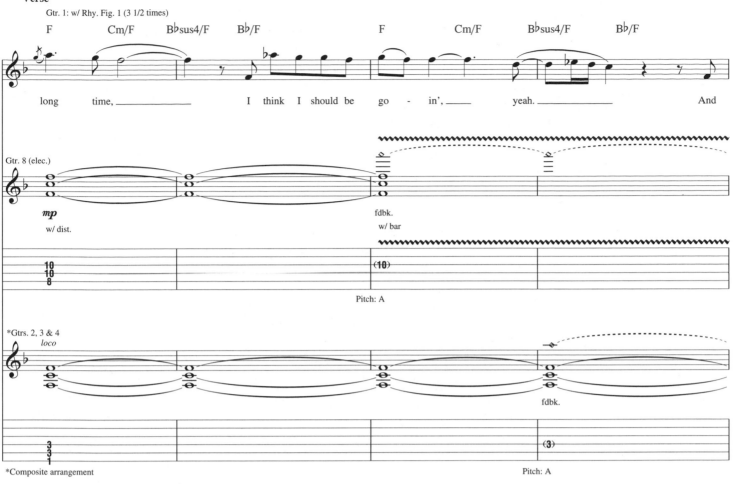

long time, _____ I think I should be go - in', ____ yeah. _____ And

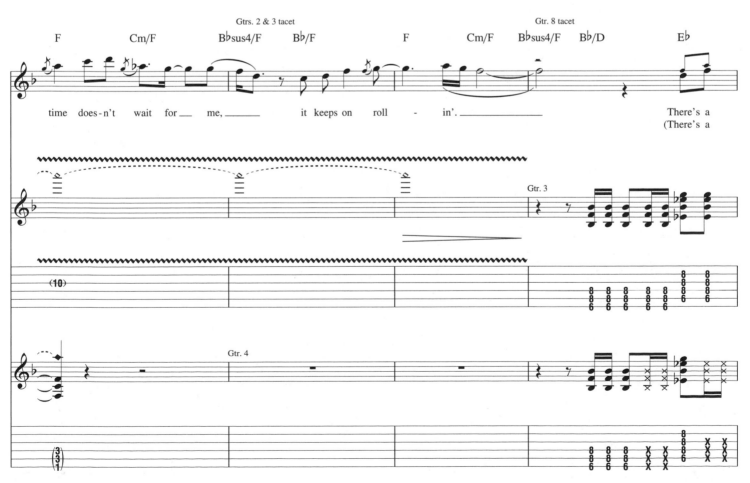

time does-n't wait for __ me, _____ it keeps on roll - in'. _____ There's a
(There's a

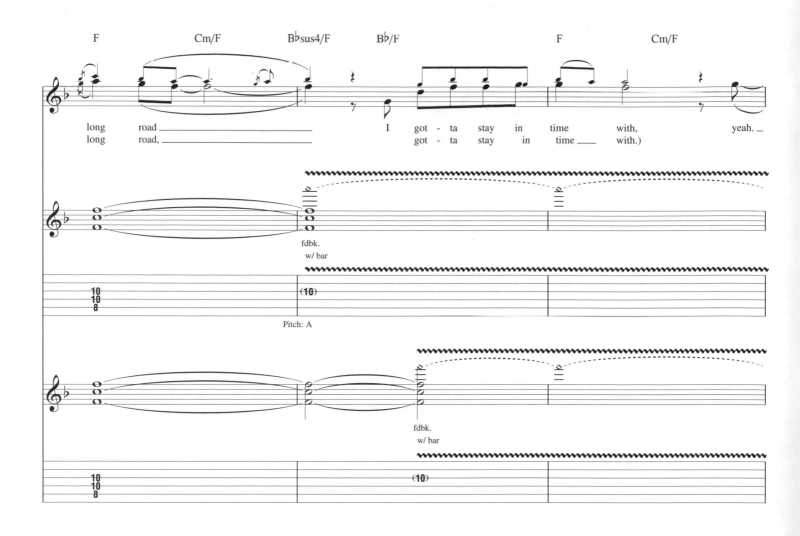

long road _____ I got-ta stay in time with,   yeah. __

long road, _____ got-ta stay in time ___ with.)

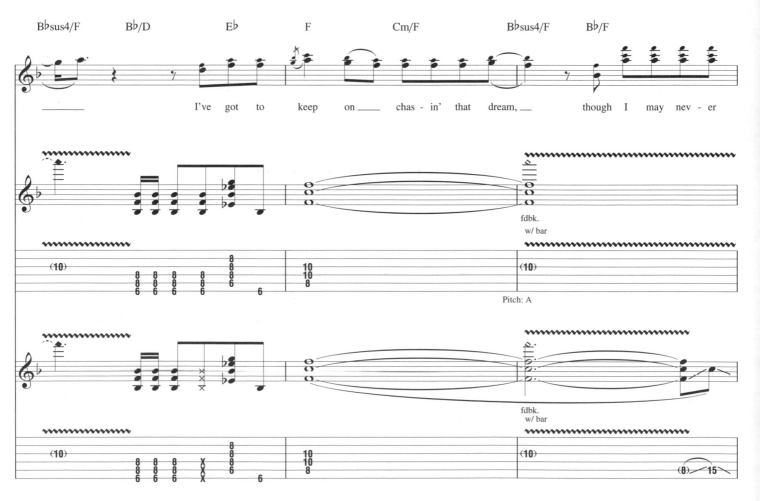

___ I've got to keep on ___ chas-in' that dream, ___ though I may nev-er

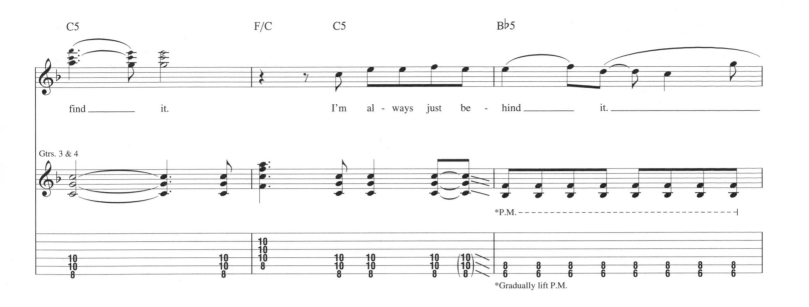

find ____ it.   I'm al - ways just be - hind ____ it. ____

Gtrs. 3 & 4

*P.M. -----------------------

*Gradually lift P.M.

Interlude

F   E♭   B♭

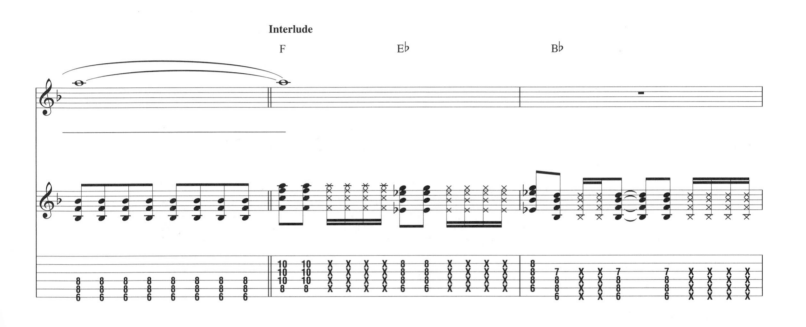

Outro

F   E♭   B♭   F   E♭

I'm just

(Well, I'm tak - in' my time, ___

Rhy. Fig. 3

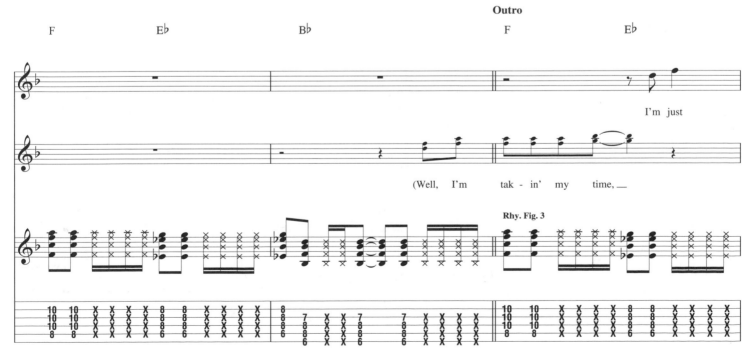

127

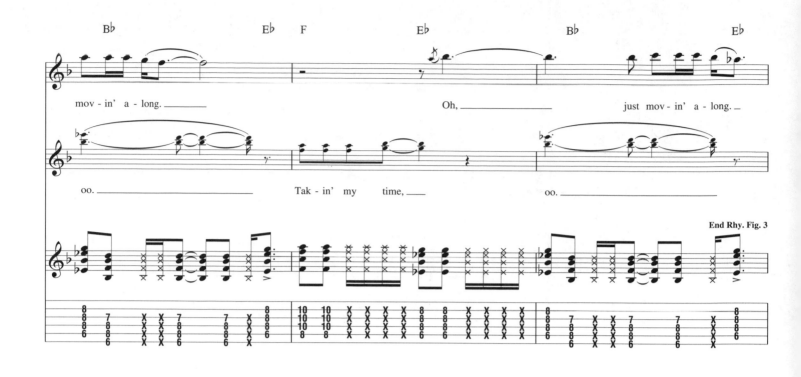

mov - in' a - long. _____   Oh, _____   just mov - in' a - long. _

oo. _____   Tak - in' my time, _____   oo. _____

End Rhy. Fig. 3

Gtrs. 3 & 4: w/ Rhy. Fig. 3 (till fade)

Ah, _____   just tak - in' my time. _____   Yeah.

Tak - in' my time, _____   oo. _____   Tak - in' my time. _____

Lead Voc.: ad lib. (till fade)

oo. _____   Tak - in' my time, _____   oo. _____

Gtr. 2

*2nd string caught under bend
finger.

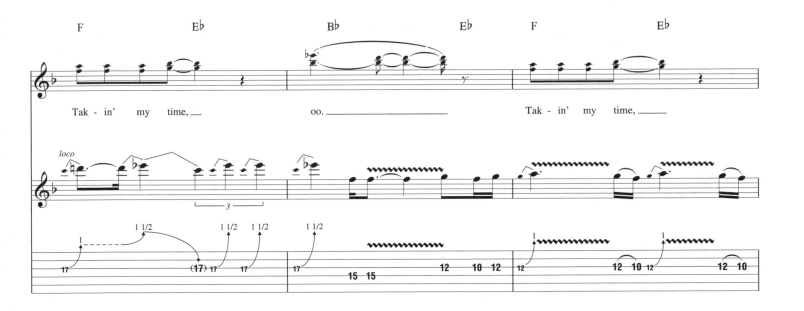

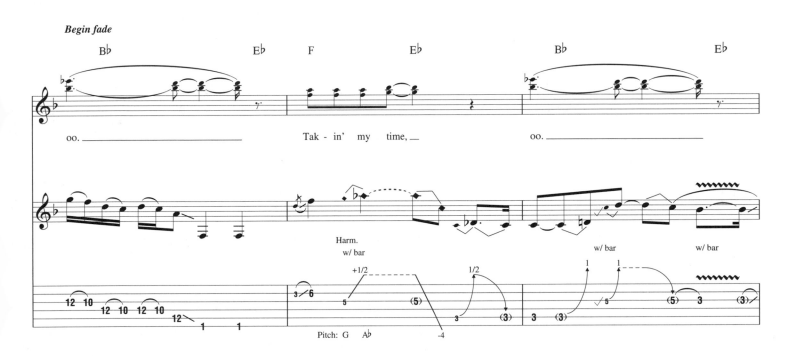

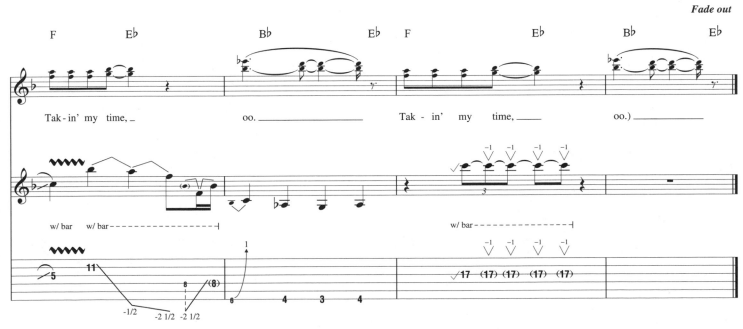

Maps

Words and Music by Karen Orzolek, Nick Zinner and Brian Chase

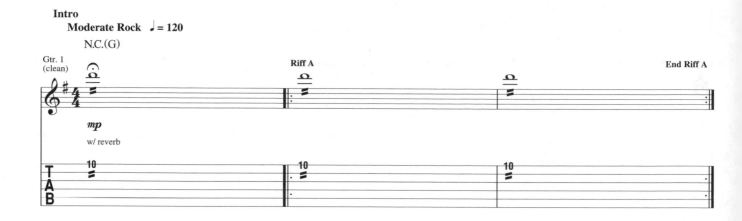

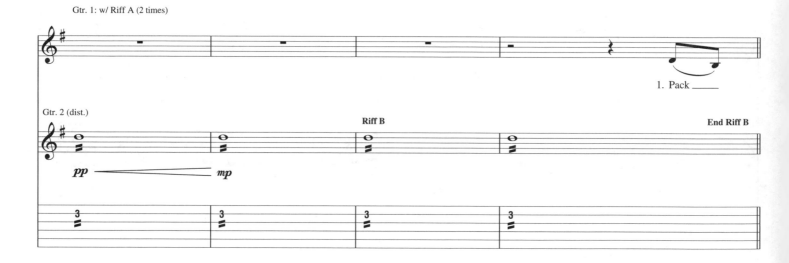

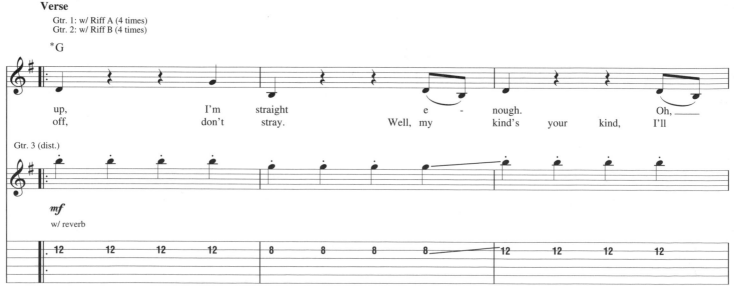

*Chord symbols reflect implied harmmony.

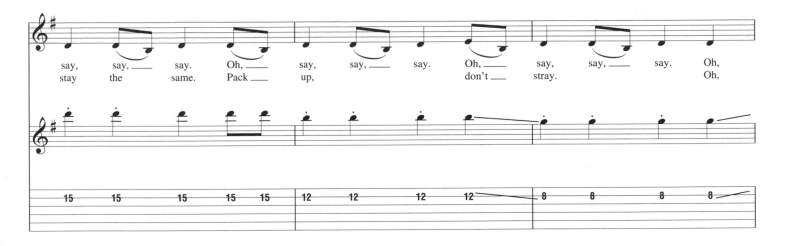

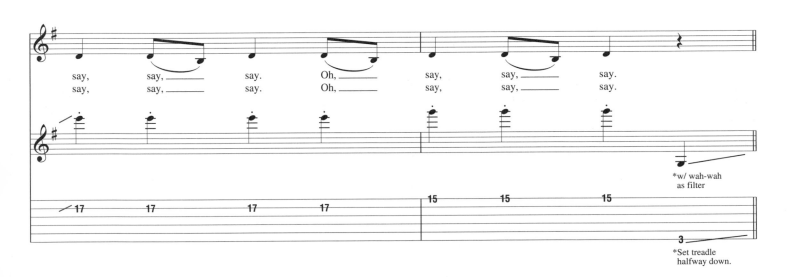

*w/ wah-wah
as filter

*Set treadle
halfway down.

𝄋 Chorus

1st time, Gtr. 1: w/ Riff A (4 times)
1st time, Gtr. 2: w/ Riff B (4 times)
2nd & 3rd times, Gtr. 1: w/ Riff A (8 times)
2nd & 3rd times, Gtr. 2: w/ Riff B (8 times)
3rd time, Gtr. 6 tacet

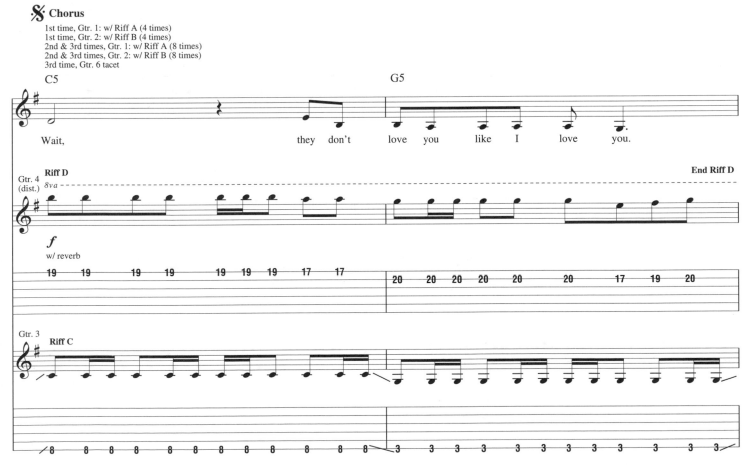

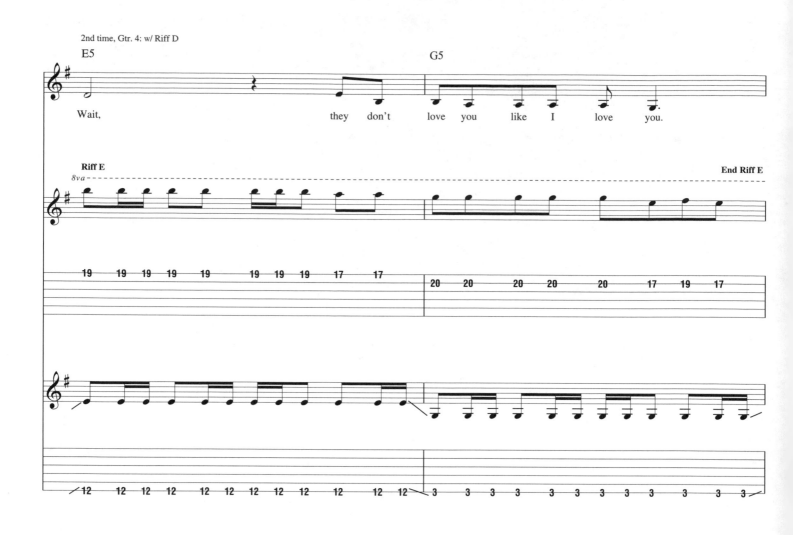

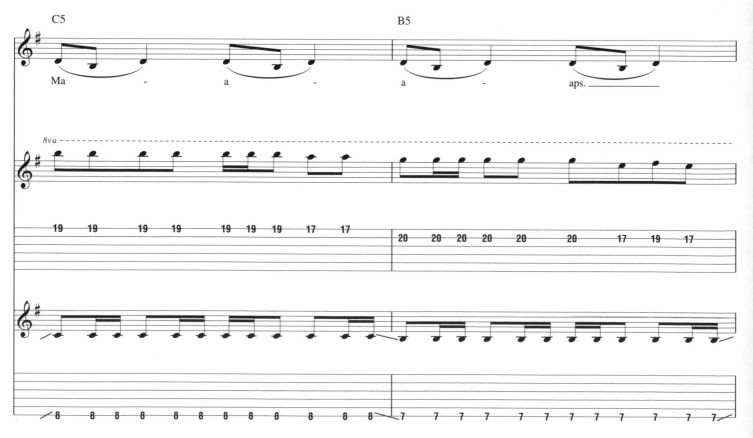

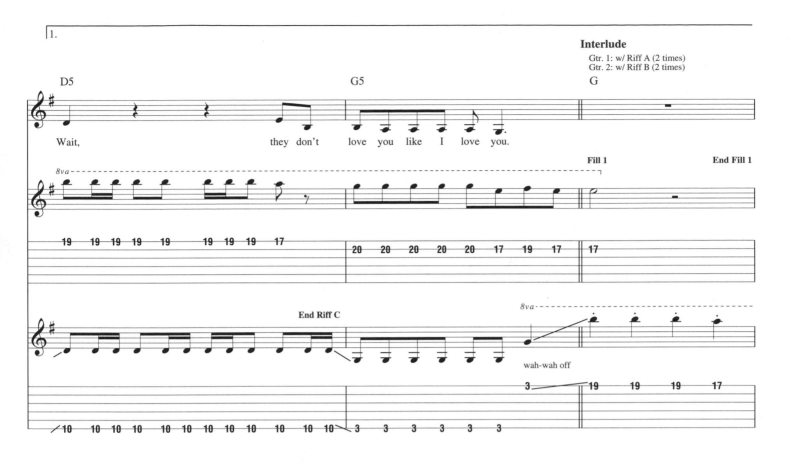

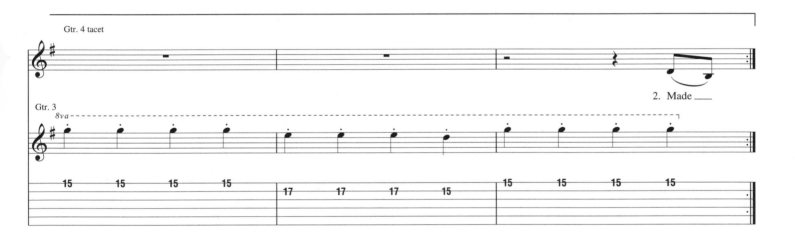

love you like I love you. Ma - a - a - aps. _____

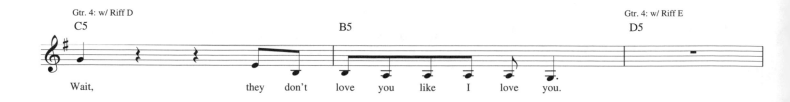

Wait, they don't love you like I love you.

Interlude

Gtr. 1: w/ Riff A (4 times)
Gtr. 2: w/ Riff B (4 times)
Gtr. 4: w/ Fill 1

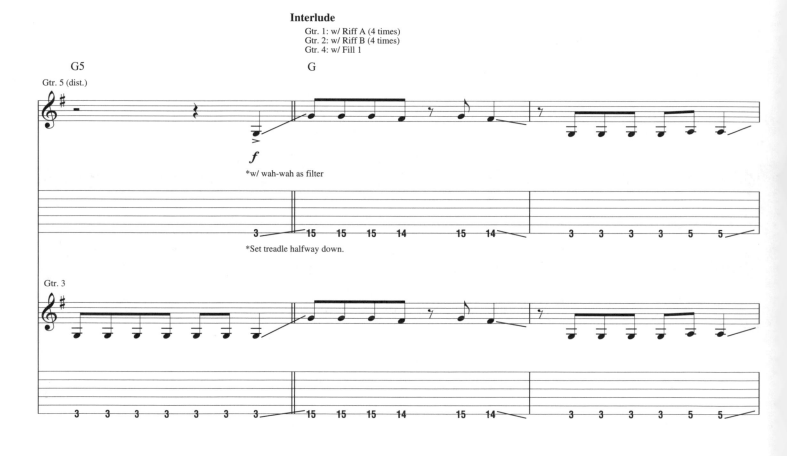

*w/ wah-wah as filter

*Set treadle halfway down.

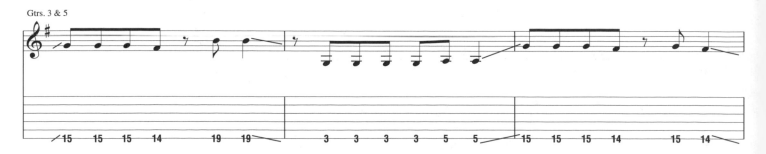

Bridge

Gtr. 1: w/ Riff A (4 times)
Gtr. 2: w/ Riff B (4 times)
Gtr. 5 tacet

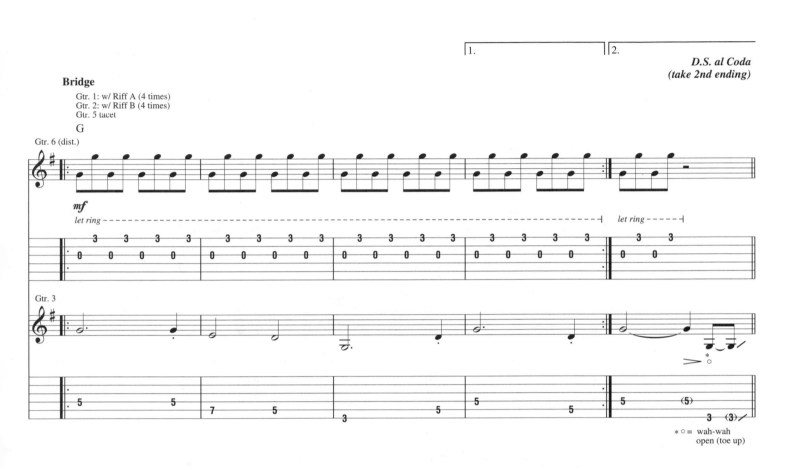

* ○ = wah-wah
open (toe up)

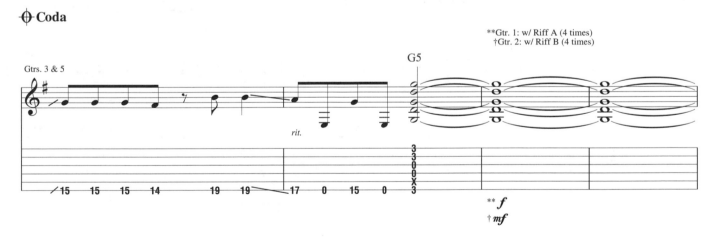

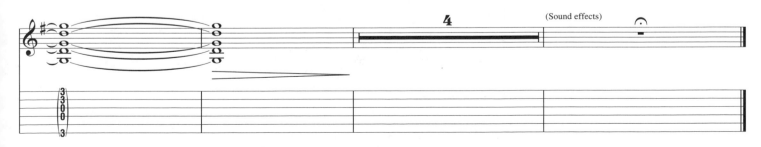

Mississippi Queen

Words and Music by Leslie West, Felix Pappalardi, Corky Laing and David Rea

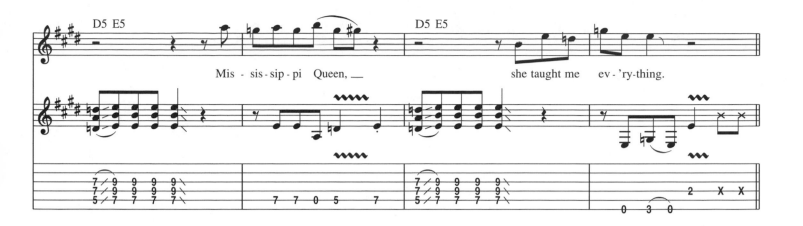

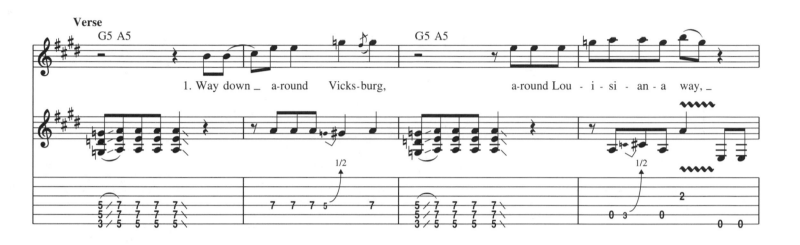

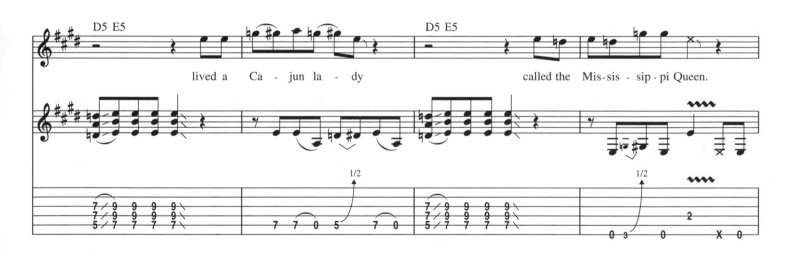

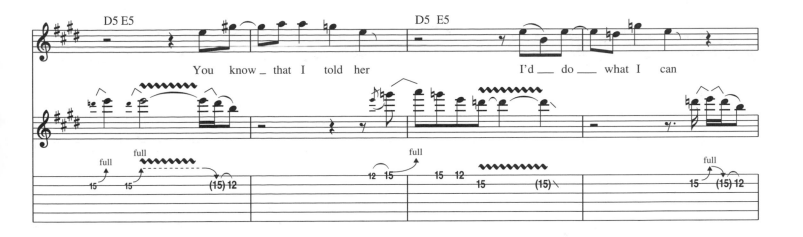

You know __ that I told her   I'd __ do __ what I can

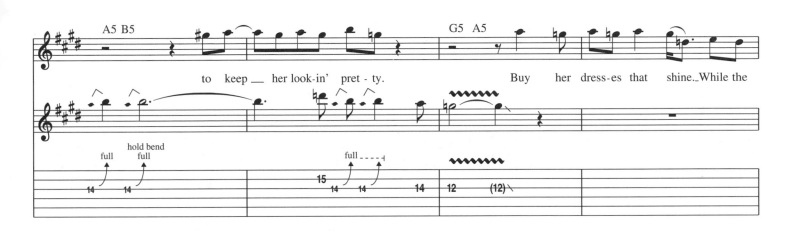

to keep __ her look-in' pret - ty.   Buy   her   dress-es that   shine.__While the

rest of them dudes was a' mak-in' their bread;   bud-dy, beg your par-don I was   los - in' mine.

Guitar Solo

Gtr. 1: w/ Rhy. Fig. 1, 1st 23 meas. only

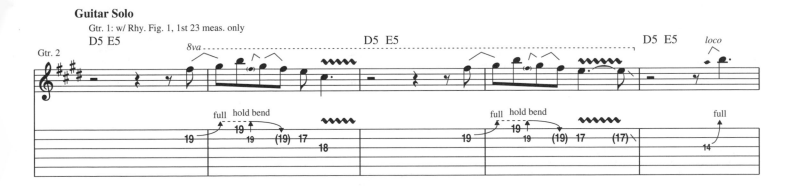

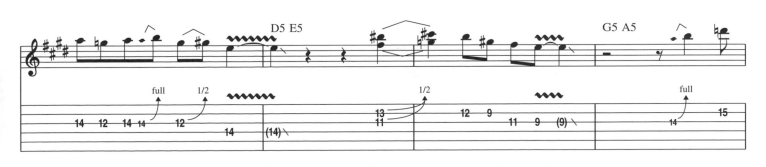

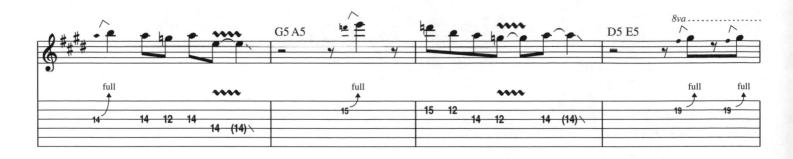

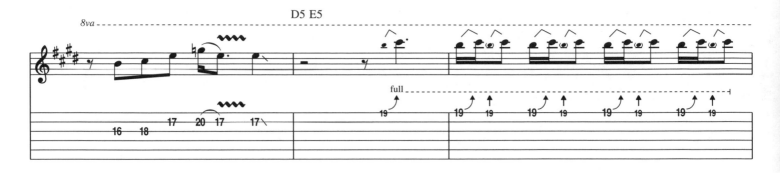

You know __ she was __ a danc - er, __ she moved __ bet - ter on wine. While the

rest of them __ dudes __ was __ get - tin' their kicks; broth-er, beg your par-don I was get-tin' mine. __

Hey, _____ Mis - sis - sip - pi Queen. __

Fill 2
Gtr. 1

Next to You

Music and Lyrics by Sting

* Note held over from previous song, "Landlord."

* Microphonic fdbk; not caused by string vibration.

Lyrics:

1. I can't stand it for an-oth-er day, when you live so man-y miles a-way. Noth-in' else is gon-na make me stay. You took me o-ver, let me find a way.

2. I sold my house, I sold my mo-tor, too. ___ next to you. I'd rob a bank, may-be steal a plane.

3. I had a thou-sand girls or may-be more, ___ this be-fore. What just hap-pened, what's come o-ver me?

All I want is to be al-though I've nev-er felt like

You took me o-ver, think I'm ___ go-in' in-sane. ___
You took me o-ver, take look ___ at ___ me. ___

What can I

New York Cit - y.

4. I saw the doc - tor he said,

"Give it time."

I've got this feel - in' gon - na lose my mind.

When all it is is just a love af - fair.

You took me o - ver, ba - by, take me there.

Paranoid

Words and Music by Anthony Iommi, John Osbourne, WIlliam Ward and Terence Butler

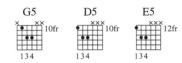

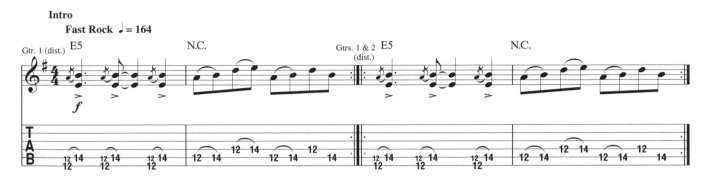

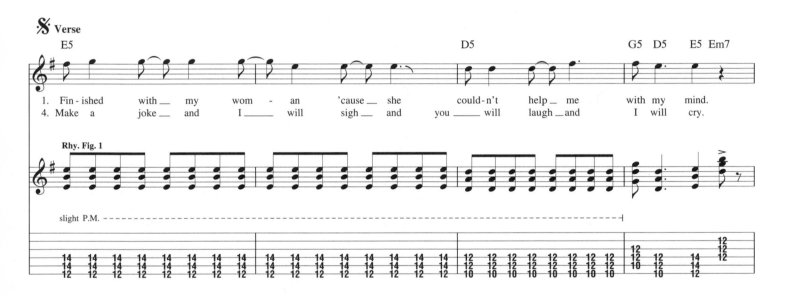

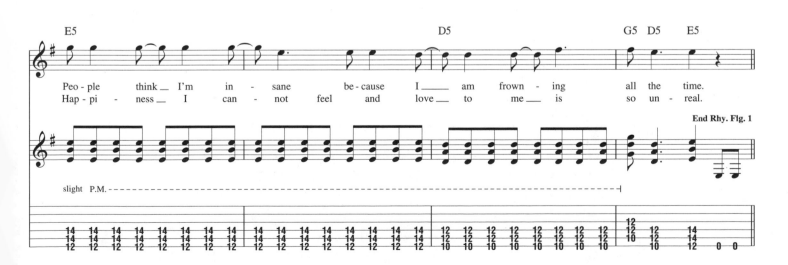

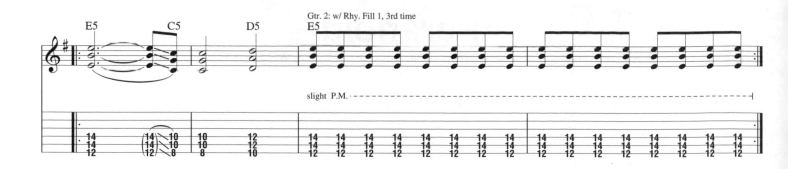

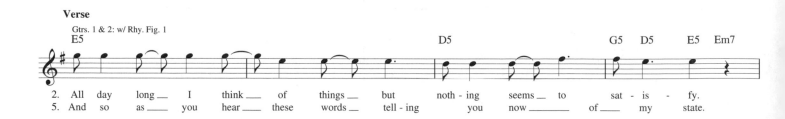

Verse

2. All day long___ I think___ of things___ but noth-ing seems___ to sat - is - fy.

5. And so as___ you hear___ these words___ tell - ing you now_____ of___ my state.

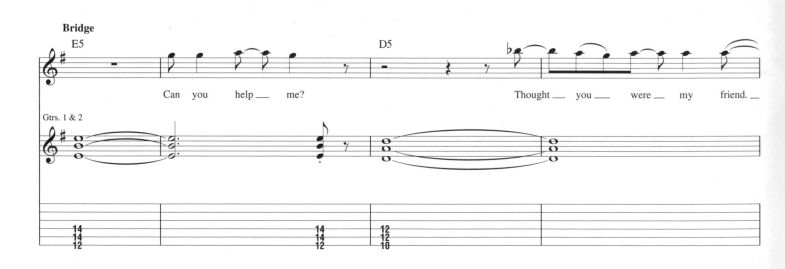

Think I'll lose___ my mind___ if I___ don't find___ some - thing___ to pass it by.

I tell you___ to en - joy life,___ I wish___ I could___ but it's too late.

Bridge

Can you help___ me?

Thought___ you___ were___ my friend.

Gtrs. 1 & 2

Whoa, _____ yeah! __

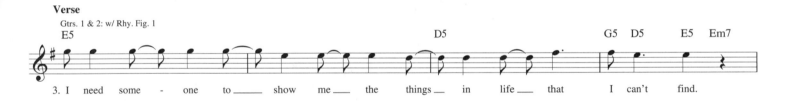

Interlude

slight P.M. --

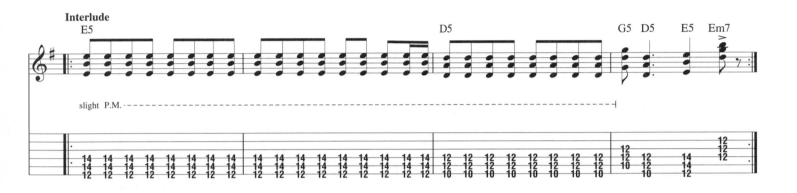

Verse

Gtrs. 1 & 2: w/ Rhy. Fig. 1

3. I need some - one to ___ show me ___ the things ___ in life ___ that I can't find.

I can't see ___ the things ___ that make ___ true hap - pi - ness, ___ I must be blind.

Guitar solo

Gtr. 2: w/ Rhy. Fig. 1, 1st 4 meas., 4 times

*Gtr. 1

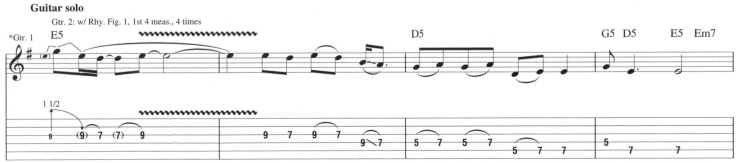

1 1/2

*With heavily distorted ring modulation effect in right channel.

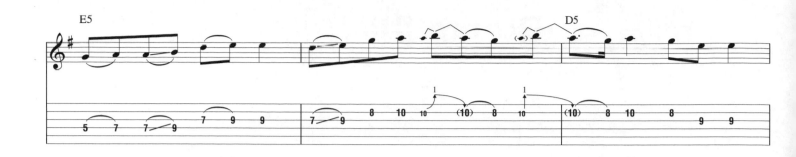

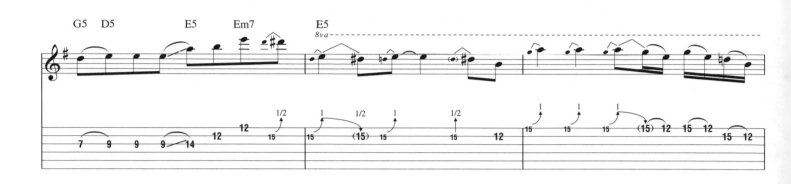

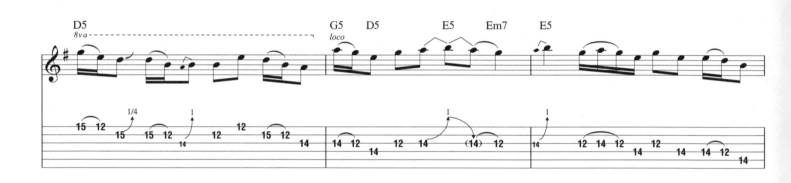

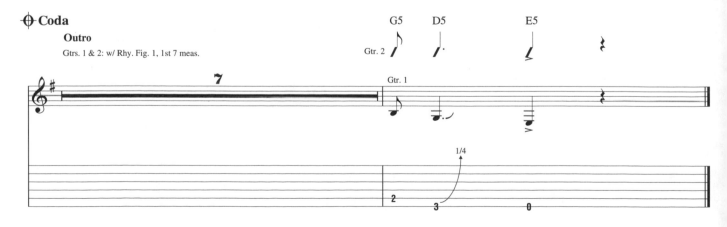

Run to the Hills

Words and Music by Steven Harris

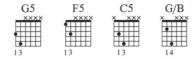

*Composite arrangement

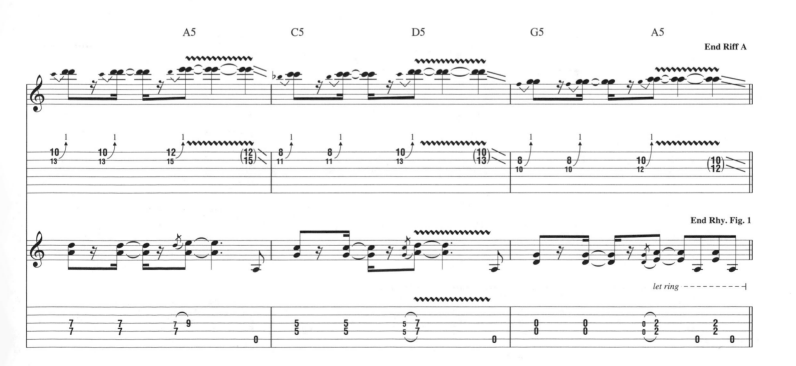

Verse

Gtrs. 1 & 2: w/ Rhy. Fig. 1 (3 3/4 times)
Gtr. 3: w/ Riff A (3 3/4 times)

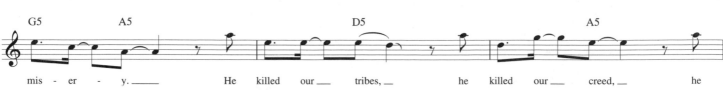

1. White man ___ came ___ a - cross the ___ sea, ___ he brought us ___ pain ___ and

mis - er - y. ___ He killed our ___ tribes, ___ he killed our ___ creed, ___ he

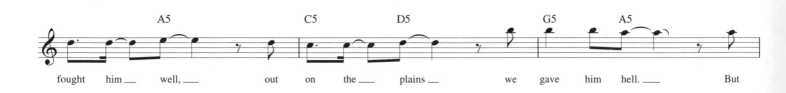

took our ___ game ___ for his own ___ need. We fought him ___ hard, ___ we

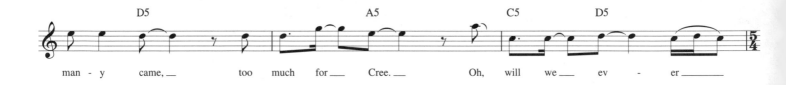

fought him ___ well, ___ out on the ___ plains ___ we gave him hell. ___ But

man - y came, ___ too much for ___ Cree. ___ Oh, will we ___ ev - er ___

Interlude

Faster ♩ = 180

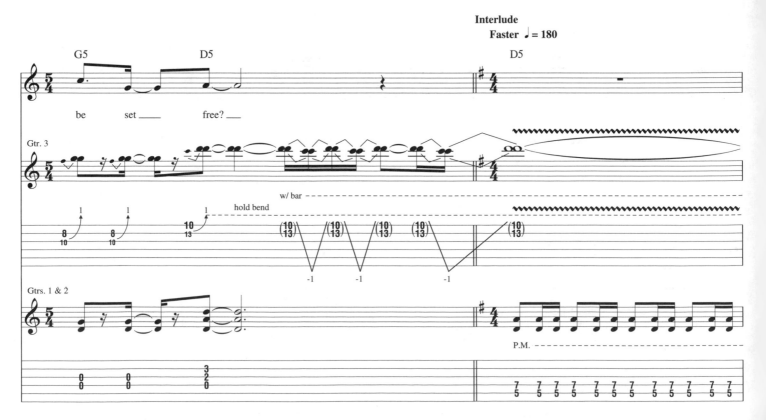

be set ___ free? ___

Gtr. 3

w/ bar

hold bend

Gtrs. 1 & 2

P.M.

Lyrics under the staves:

Mur - der for free - dom, a stab in the back, wom - en and chil - dren and
Sell - ing them whis - key and tak - ing their gold, en - slav - ing the young and de -

cow - ards at - tack. _____ Run
stroy - ing the old. _____

to the hills,

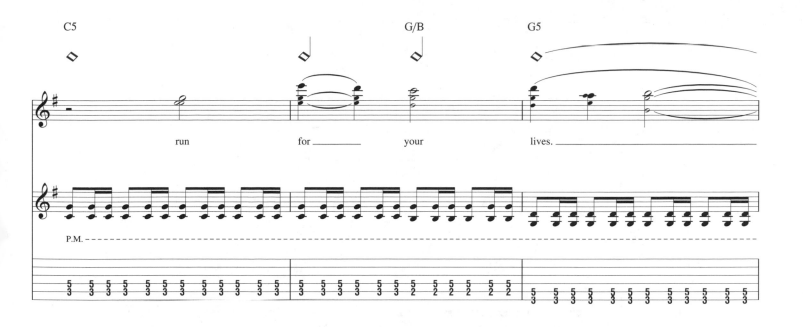

run   for _____ your   lives. _____

Gtrs. 1 & 2: w/ Rhy. Figs. 2 & 2A (1st 6 meas.)

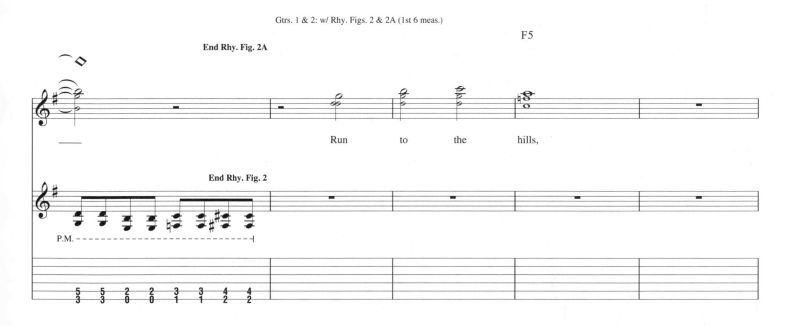

Run   to   the   hills,

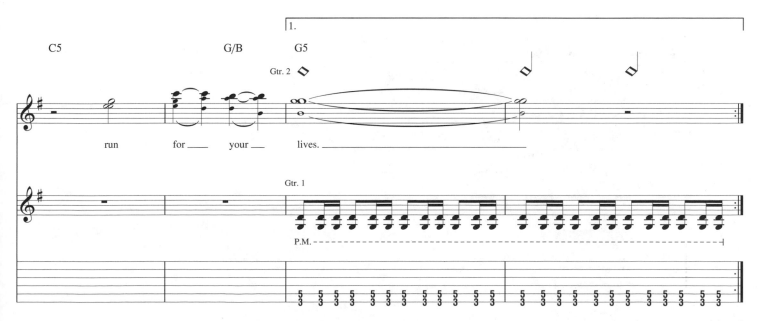

run   for ___ your ___ lives. _____

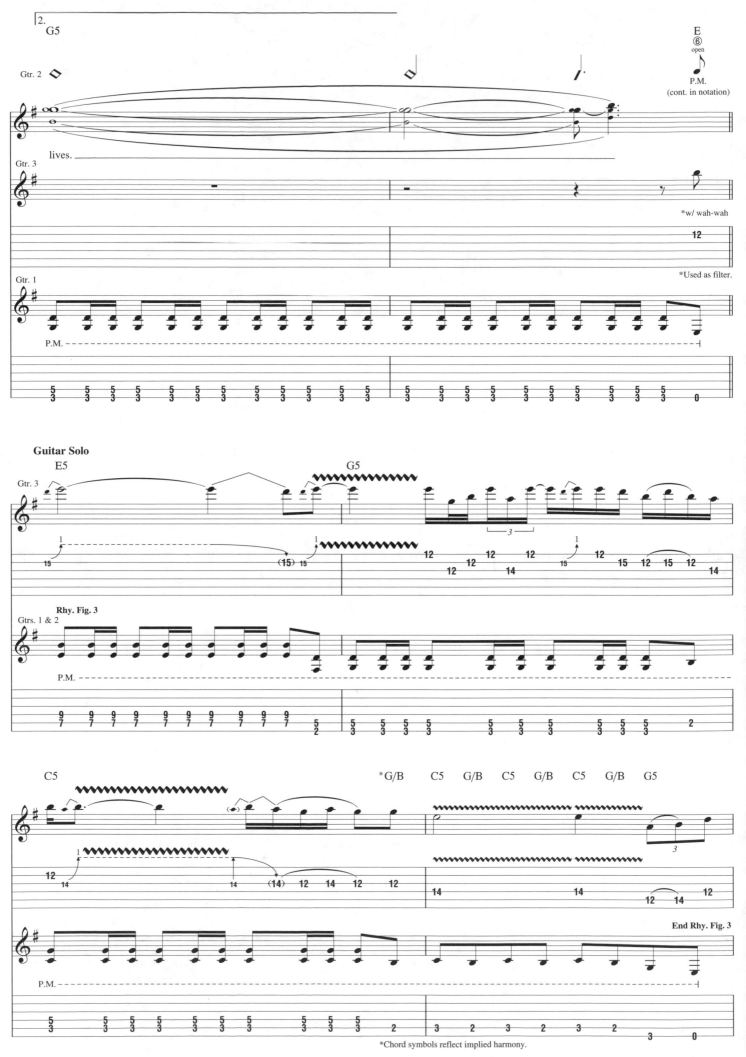

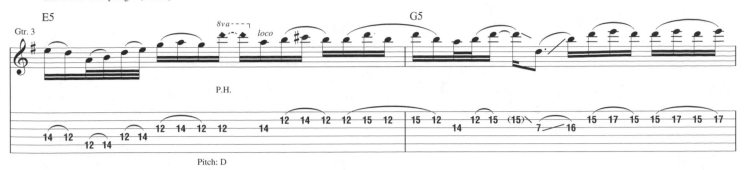

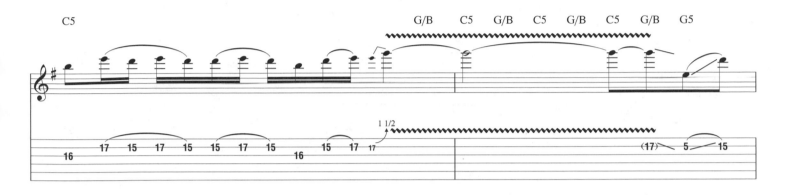

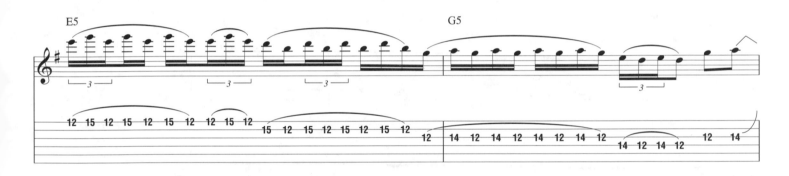

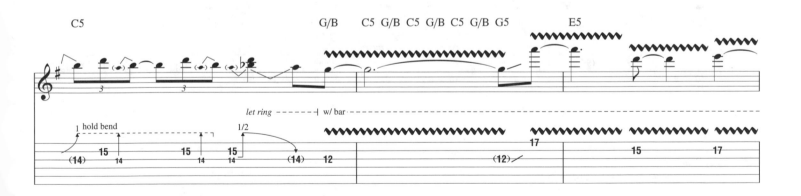

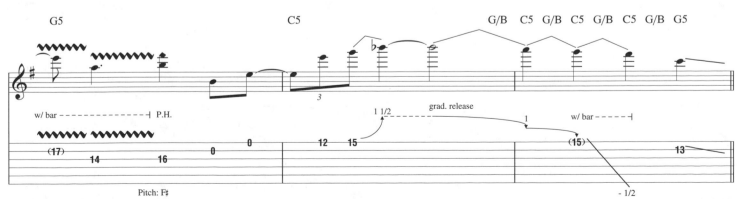

Interlude

1st time, Gtr. 3 tacet

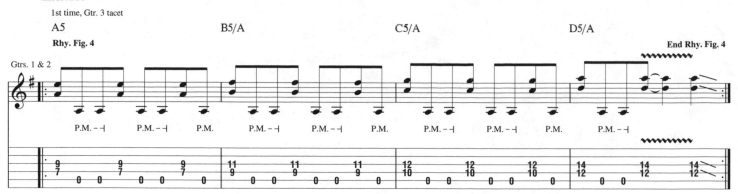

Gtrs. 1 & 2: w/ Rhy. Fig. 4

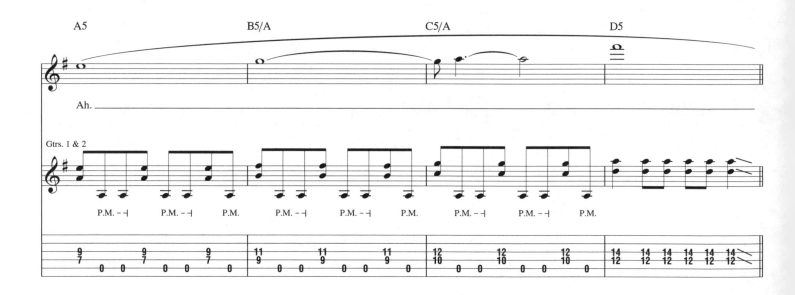

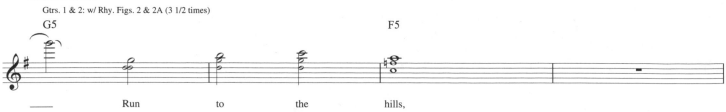

Outro-Chorus

Gtrs. 1 & 2: w/ Rhy. Figs. 2 & 2A (3 1/2 times)

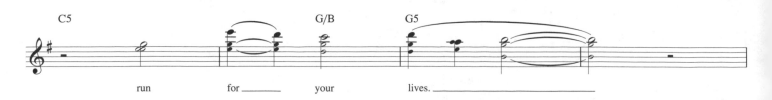

Run to the hills,

run for your lives.

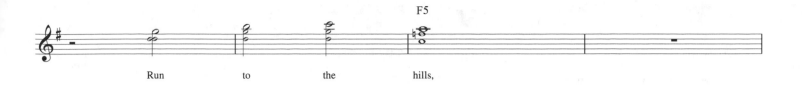

F5

Run   to   the   hills,

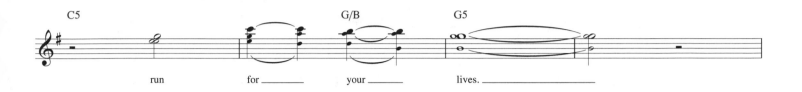

C5   G/B   G5

run   for _____ your _____ lives. _____

F5

Run   to   the   hills,

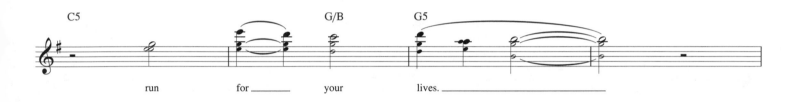

C5   G/B   G5

run   for _____ your   lives. _____

F5

Run   to   the   hills,

Free time

C5   G/B   G5

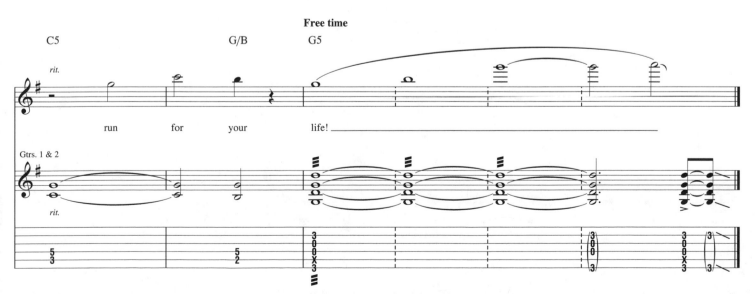

run   for   your   life! _____

Gtrs. 1 & 2

Say It Ain't So

Words and Music by Rivers Cuomo

*Two gtrs. arr. for one.   **Microphonic fdbk., not caused by string vibration.

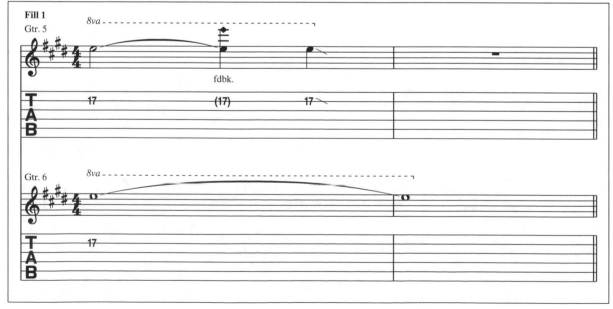

Guitar Solo

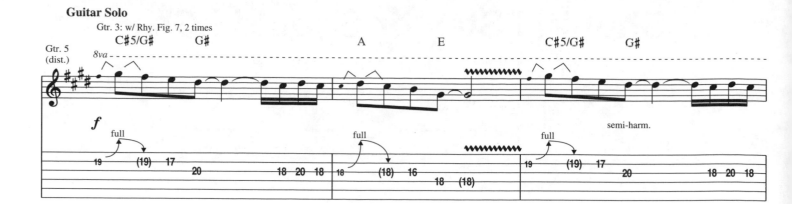

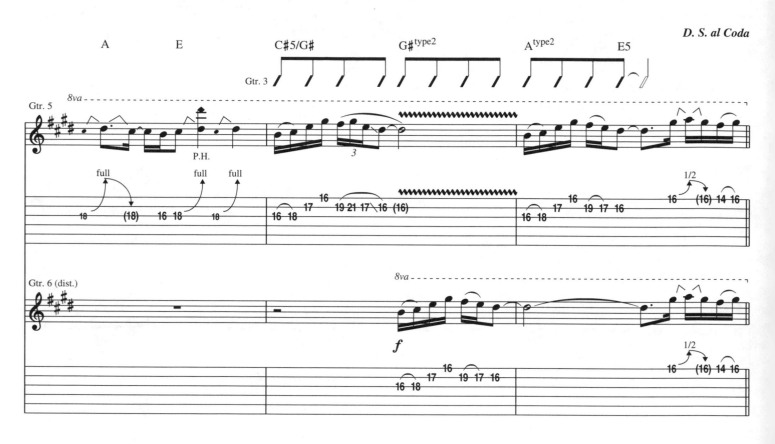

⊕ Coda

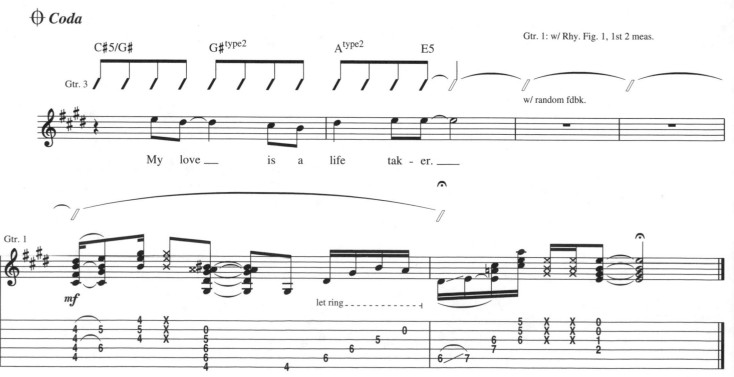

My love ___ is a life tak-er. ___

Should I Stay or Should I Go

Words and Music by Mick Jones and Joe Strummer

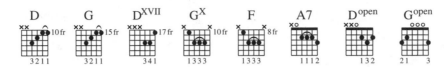

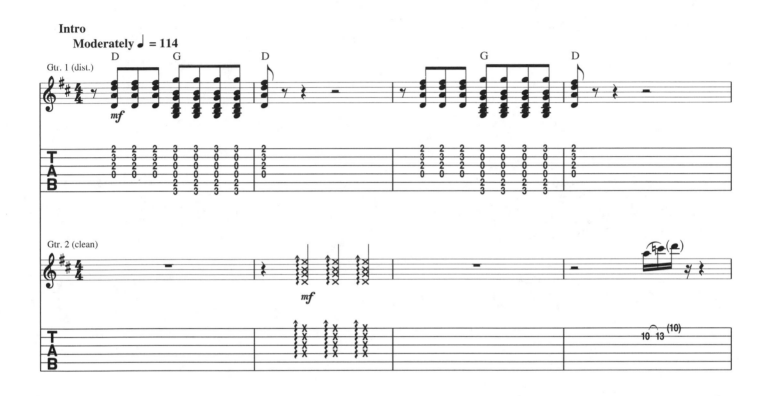

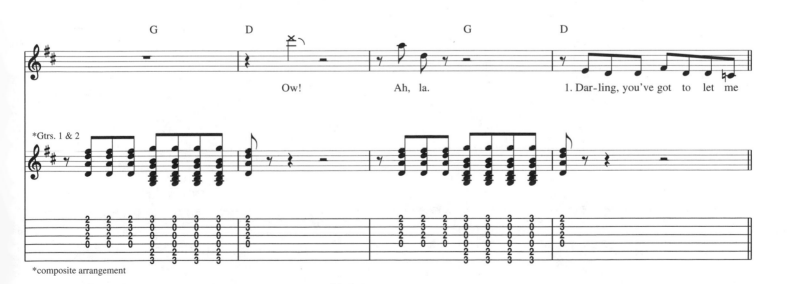

*composite arrangement

% Verse

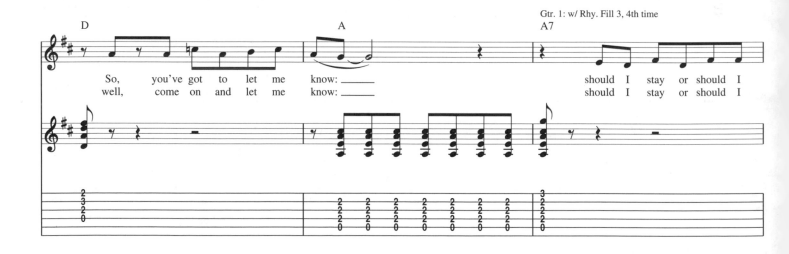

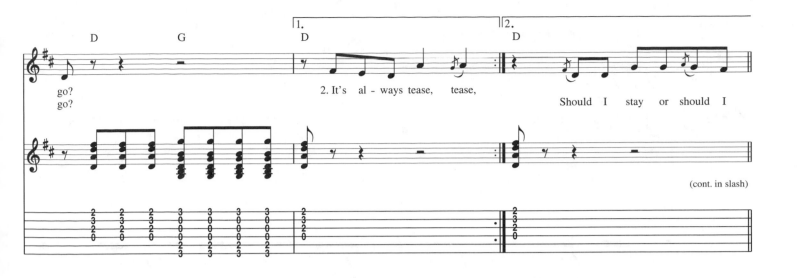

go?
go?

2. It's al - ways tease, tease,

Should I stay or should I

(cont. in slash)

Chorus
Double-Time Feel

simile on repeat

go now?
(Ten - go fri - o por el so - plo.

Should I stay or should I go now?

Ten - go fri - o por el

*Bkgd. voc. 2nd time only.

so - plo.

If I go, there will be trou - ble,

Si me voy - va a ser pe - li - gro.

and if I stay, it will be

To Coda

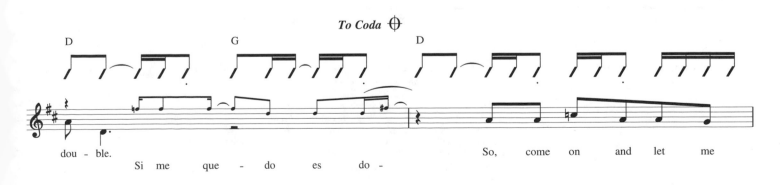

dou - ble.

Si me que - do es do -

So, come on and let me

167

End Double-Time Feel

know. _____

3. This in - de - ci - sion's bug - gin'

⊕ *Coda*

- ble.

So, you've got to let me know: _____

Me ti - en - es que de - cir.

should I cool it or should I

Outro-Chorus

Gtrs. 1 & 2: w/ Rhy. Fig. 1, simile

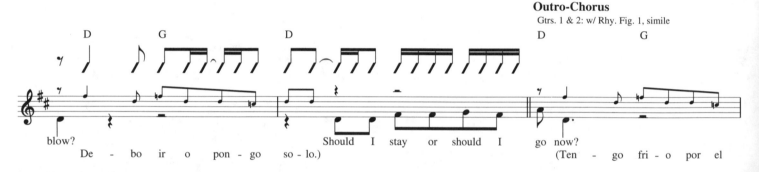

blow?

De - bo ir o pon - go so - lo.)

Should I stay or should I go now?

(Ten - go fri - o por el

so - plo.

If I go, there will be trou - ble,

Si me voy__ va a ser pe - li - gro.

and if I stay, it will be

dou - ble.

Si me que - do__ es do - ble.

So, you've got to let me know: _____

Me ti - en - es que de -

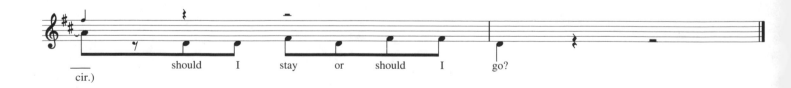

cir.)

should I stay or should I go?

Additional Lyrics

3. This indecision's buggin' me. *(Indecisión me molesta.)*
   If you don't want me, set me free. *(Si no me quieres líbrame.)*
   Exactly who I'm s'pose to be? *(Dígame que tengo ser.)*
   Don't you know which clothes even fit me? *(Sabes que ropa me queda?)*
   Come on and let me know: *(Me tienes que decir.)*
   Should I cool it or should I blow? *(Me debo ir o quedarme?)*

4. *Instrumental (w/ Voc. ad lib.)*

Suffragette City

Words and Music by David Bowie

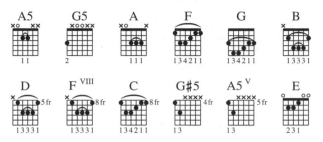

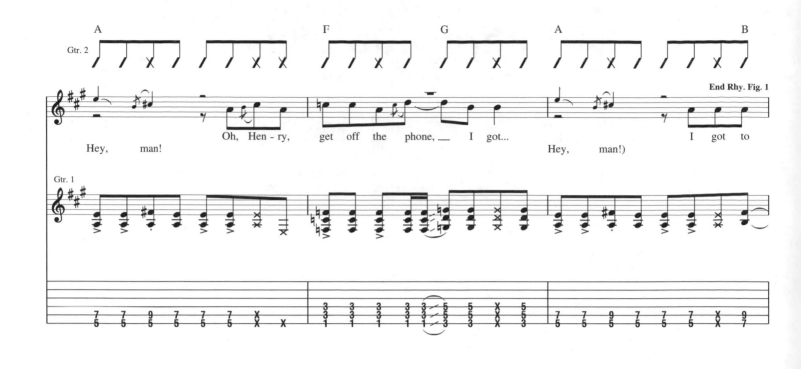

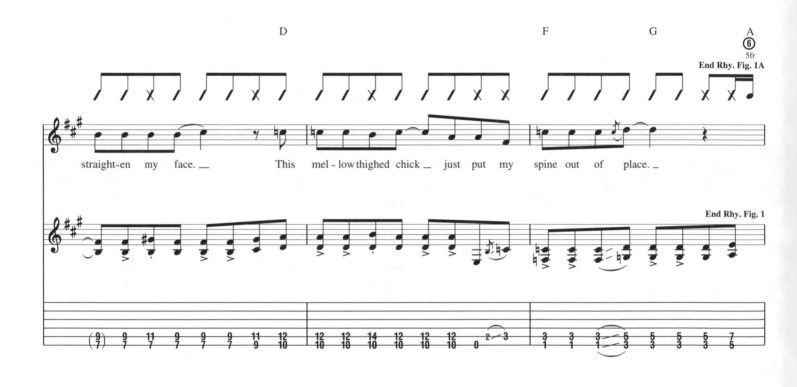

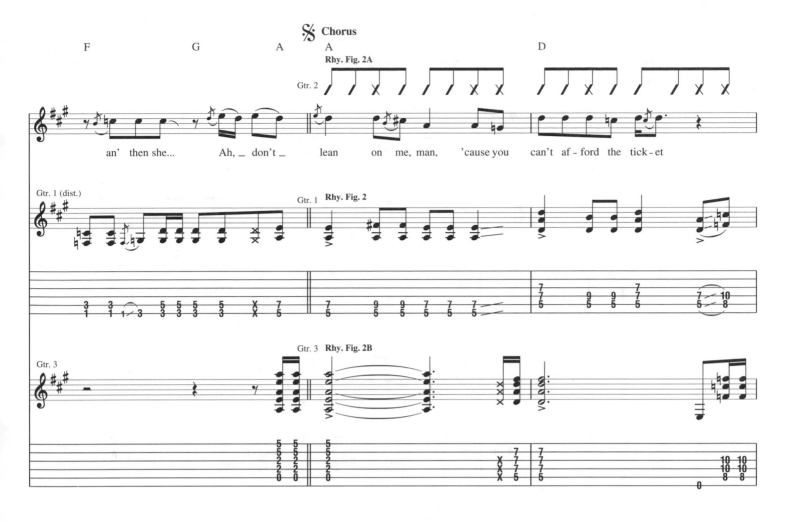

ain't got time   to check it.   You know my Suf - fra - gette Cit - y   is out - ta

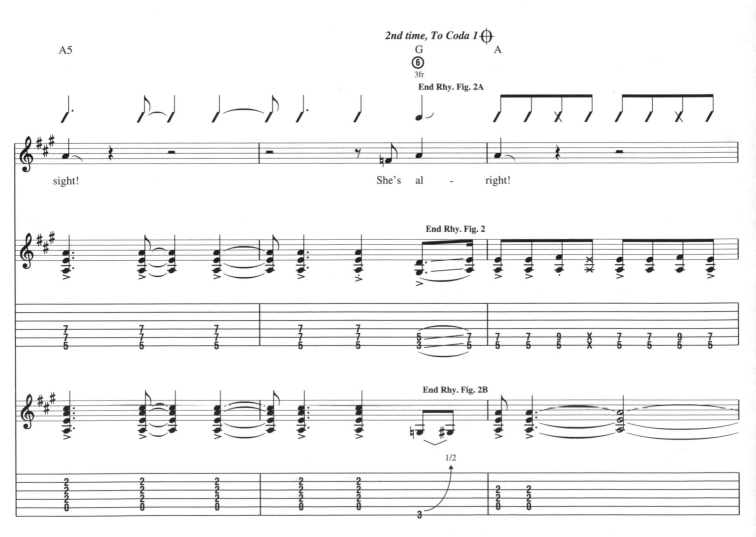

sight!   She's al - right!

Verse

Bkgd. Voc.: w/ Voc. Fig. 1
Gtrs. 1 & 2: w/ Rhy. Figs. 1 & 1A
Gtr. 3: tacet

2. Ah, Hen - ry, don't be un - kind, ___ go 'way! I can't take ___

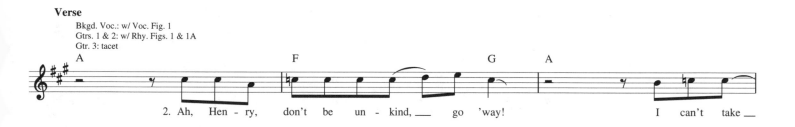

___ you this time, ___ no way! ___ Di - droog - ie, don't crash here. ___ There's

D.S. al Coda 1

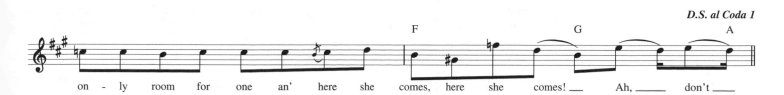

on - ly room for one an' here she comes, here she comes! ___ Ah, ___ don't ___

173

Uh, don't _

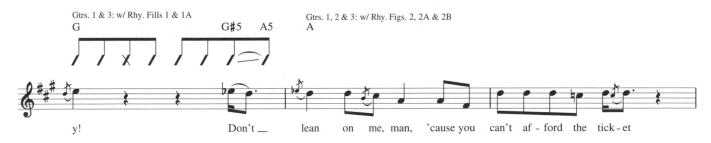

⊕ Coda 2

Gtrs. 1 & 3: w/ Rhy. Fills 1 & 1A

Gtrs. 1, 2 & 3: w/ Rhy. Figs. 2, 2A & 2B

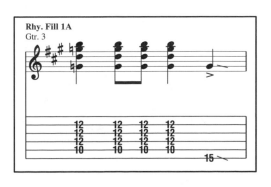

y!   Don't _   lean   on   me, man, 'cause you   can't af - ford   the tick - et

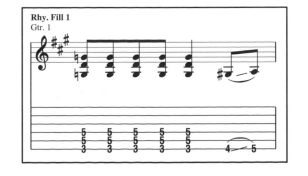

back from Suf-fra-gette Cit - y! Un, don't_ lean on me, man, 'cause you ain't got time to check it.

You know my Suf-fra-gette Cit - y is out-ta sight! Wa!_____ she's al -

Outro

right!   My Suf-fra-gette Cit - y!   My Suf-fra-gette Cit -

Gtrs. 1, 2 & 3: w/ Rhy. Figs. 3 & 3A & 3B (2 3/4 times)

y!   I'm back from Suf-fra-gette Cit - y!   I'm back from Suf-fra-gette Cit -

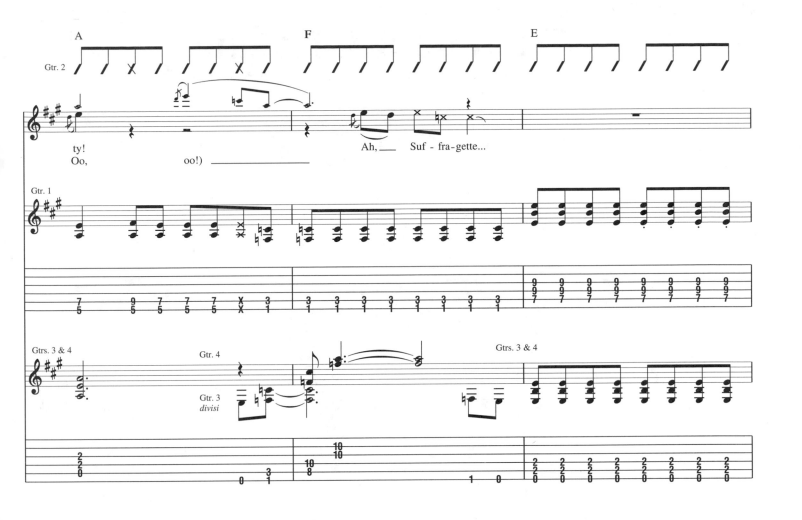

ty!
Oo, oo!)

Ah, ___ Suf - fra-gette...

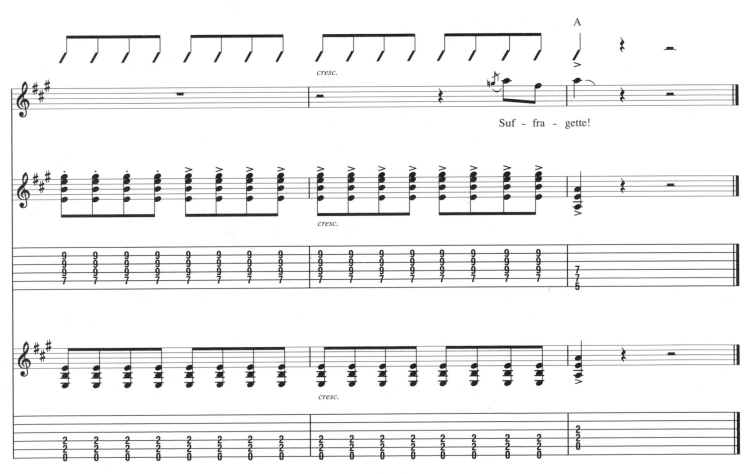

cresc.

Suf - fra - gette!

cresc.

cresc.

Train Kept A-Rollin'

Words and Music by Tiny Bradshaw, Lois Mann and Howie Kay

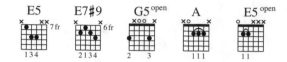

Verse

train, I met a dame. She was rath - er hand - some; we kind - a looked the same. _ She was

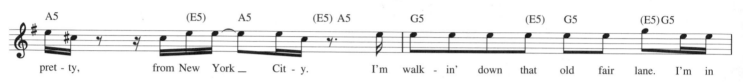

pret - ty, from New York _ Cit - y. I'm walk - in' down that old fair lane. I'm in

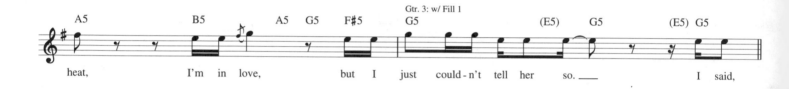

heat, I'm in love, but I just could - n't tell her so. _ I said,

Chorus

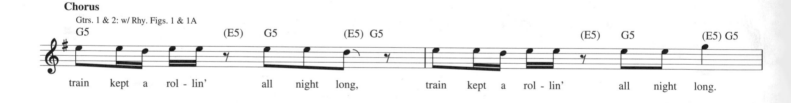

train kept a rol - lin' all night long, train kept a rol - lin' all night long.

Train kept a rol - lin' all night long, train kept a rol - lin' all night long, with a

heave _ and a ho, but I just could - n't tell her so. _ No, _ no,

182

* Str. is still bent 1/2 step after pulling off.

* Studio trickery creates the illusion of a live performance.

188

Guitar Solo

but I just could-n't tell her so. ___ I said,

Chorus

train kept a rol-lin' all ___ night long, train kept a rol-lin'

Wanted Dead or Alive

Words and Music by Jon Bon Jovi and Richie Sambora

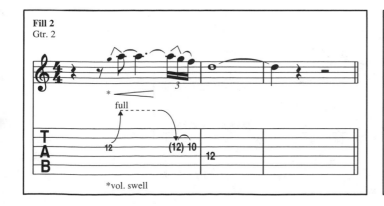
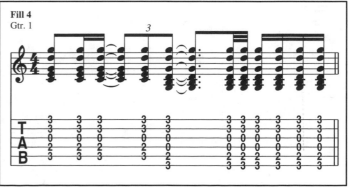

Gtr. 2: w/ Fill 6, 3rd time

fac - es are_ so cold,   I'd drive all   night _____   just to get back_ home. _
bot - tle that_ you drink.   And times when you're a - lone, __   all you do is think.
stand - ing __ tall, ___   I've seen a mil - lion fac - es,   and I've rocked them all.___   I'm a

End Rhy. Fig. 1

Chorus

Gtr. 2: w/ Fill 5, 2nd time

cow - boy,   on a steel _ horse_ I ride.   I'm want - ed,   (want - ed, __)

sing 2nd & 3rd times only

Rhy. Fig. 2

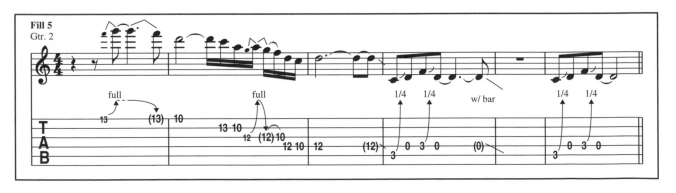

Fill 5
Gtr. 2

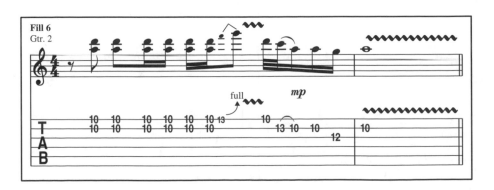

Fill 6
Gtr. 2

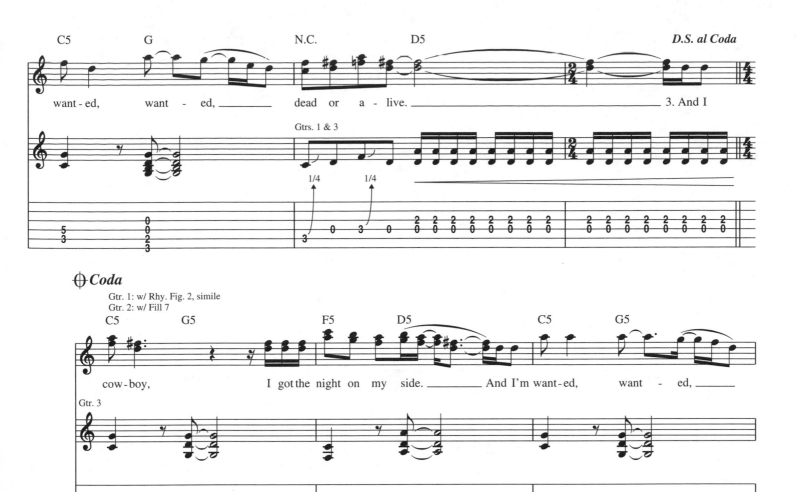

want - ed,   want - ed, _____ dead or a - live. _____ 3. And I

⊕ *Coda*

Gtr. 1: w/ Rhy. Fig. 2, simile
Gtr. 2: w/ Fill 7

cow-boy,   I got the night on my side. _____ And I'm want-ed,   want - ed, _____

Gtr. 1: w/ Rhy. Fig. 2, last 2 meas., simile

dead or a - live, __ dead or a - live, ____ dead or a - live, _____ dead or a - live. __ I still

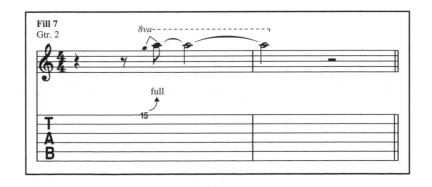

Fill 7
Gtr. 2

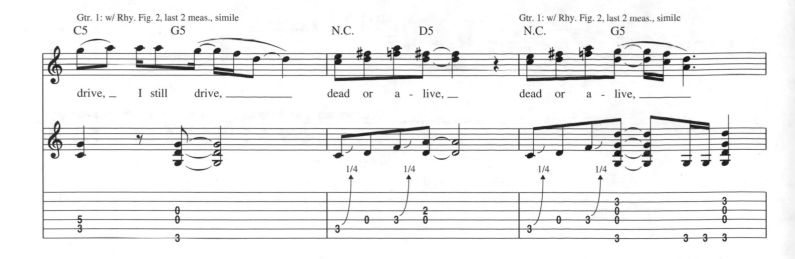

drive, __ I still drive, _____ dead or a - live, __ dead or a - live, _____

dead or a - live, __ dead or a - live, _____ dead or a - live. _____

Gtrs. 1 & 3

Outro

Gtr. 3 tacet

N.C.

Gtr. 1

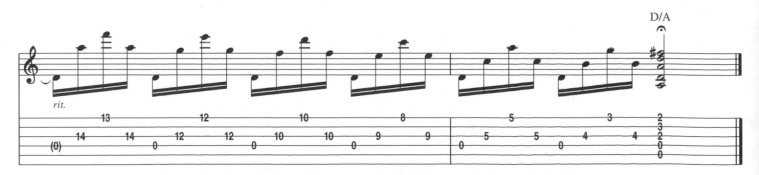

rit.

D/A

Welcome Home

Words and Music by Claudio Sanchez, Michael Todd, Joshua Eppard and Travis Stever

Tune down 1/2 step:
(low to high) E♭-A♭-D♭-G♭-B♭-E♭

*Chord symbols reflect implied harmony.

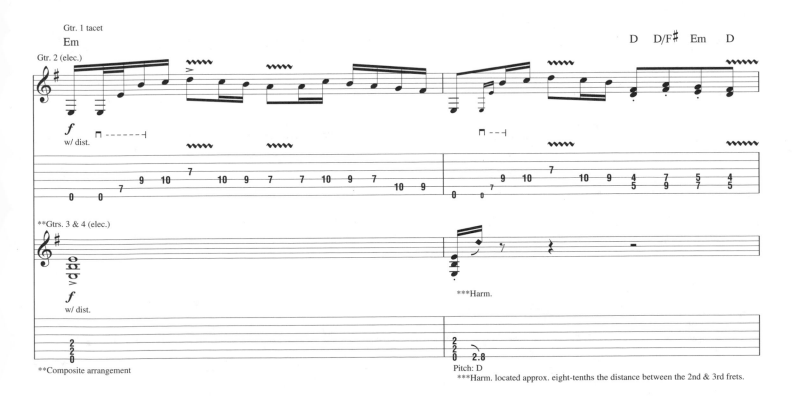

**Composite arrangement

Pitch: D

***Harm. located approx. eight-tenths the distance between the 2nd & 3rd frets.

Pitch: A

Pitch: F#   B

*Microphonic fdbk., not caused by string vibration.

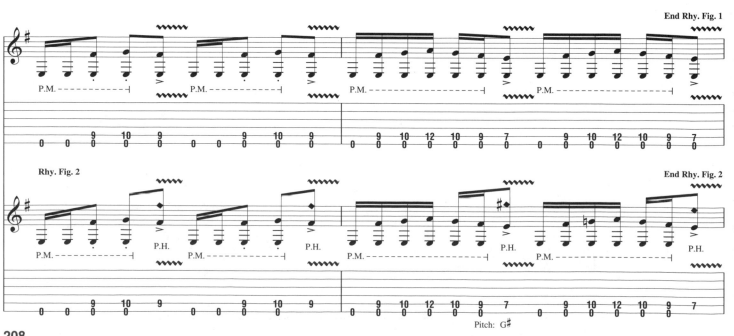

Pitch: G#

208

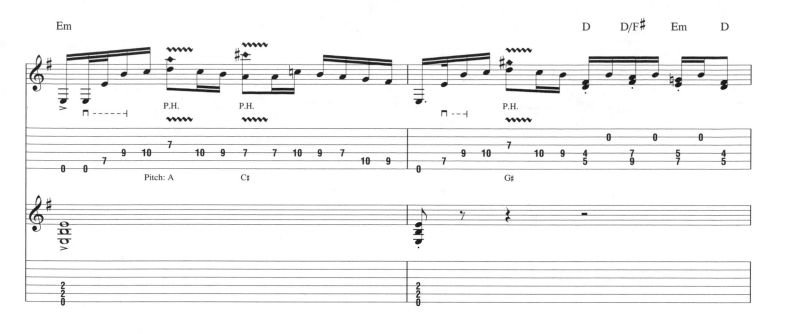

Gtr. 4: w/ Rhy. Fill 1

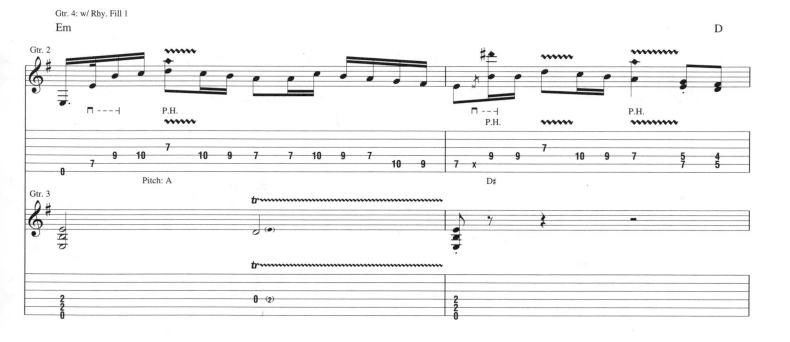

Gtr. 2: w/ Rhy. Fig. 1
Gtrs. 3 & 4: w/ Rhy. Fig. 2 (2 times)

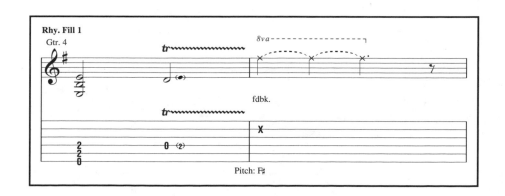

Verse

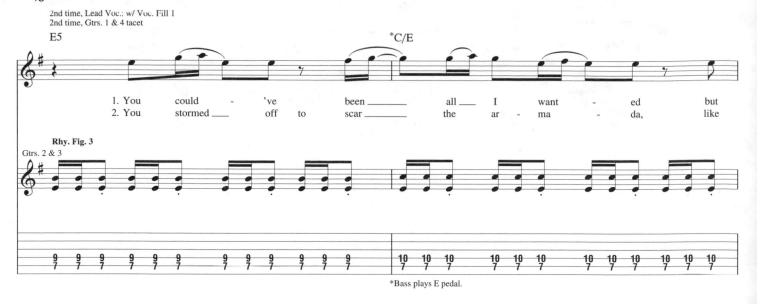

2nd time, Lead Voc.: w/ Voc. Fill 1
2nd time, Gtrs. 1 & 4 tacet

E5   *C/E

1. You could-'ve been _____ all _____ I want-ed but
2. You stormed _____ off to scar _____ the ar-ma-da, like

Rhy. Fig. 3
Gtrs. 2 & 3

*Bass plays E pedal.

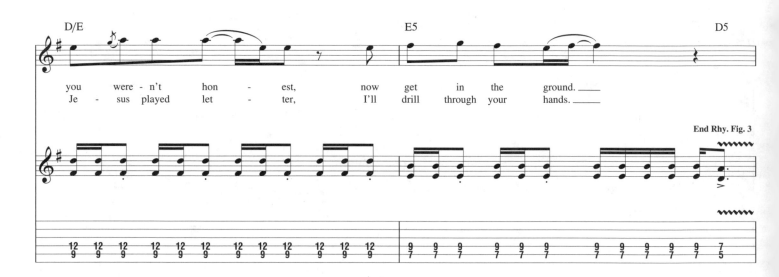

D/E   E5   D5

you were-n't hon - est, now get in the ground. _____
Je - sus played let - ter, I'll drill through your hands. _____

End Rhy. Fig. 3

Gtrs. 2 & 3: w/ Rhy. Fig. 3 (3 times)

E5   C/E   D/E

You choked _____ off the sur - est of fa - vors _____ but if you real - ly love _____ me you
The stone _____ for the curse _____ you have blamed _____ me. With love and de - vo - tion, I'll

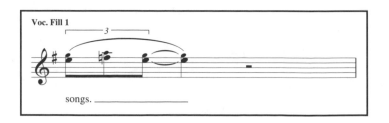

Voc. Fill 1

_3_

songs. _____

210

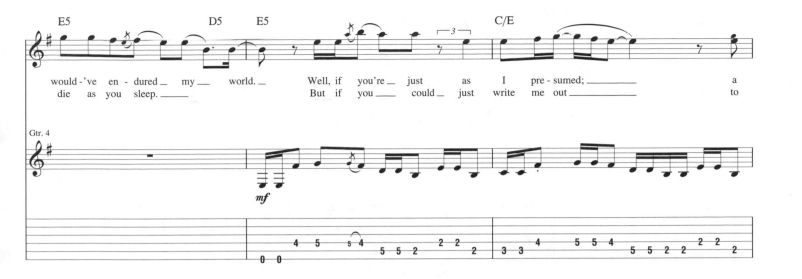

would-'ve en - dured __ my __ world. __   Well, if   you're __   just   as   I   pre - sumed; _____   a
die   as   you   sleep. ____   But   if   you __   could __   just   write   me   out _____   to

Gtr. 4

D/E

whore   in   sheep's   cloth - ing, __   fuck - ing   up   all   I   do. _____   And __   it's ____   all __
nev - er - less   won - der, __   hap - py   will   I   be - come. ____   Be __   true ____   that __

To Coda ⊕

C/E

here _____   we   stop ____   then   nev - er   a - gain ____   will   you   see   this   in   your __   life. __
this   is   no - op - tion. ____   So   with   sin, I   con - demn __   you. __   De - mon   play, de - mon __   out. __

Chorus

Hang on ___ to the glo - ry at my ___ right hand. ___

Here ___ laid to ___ rest, ___ is our love ___ ev - er longed? ___

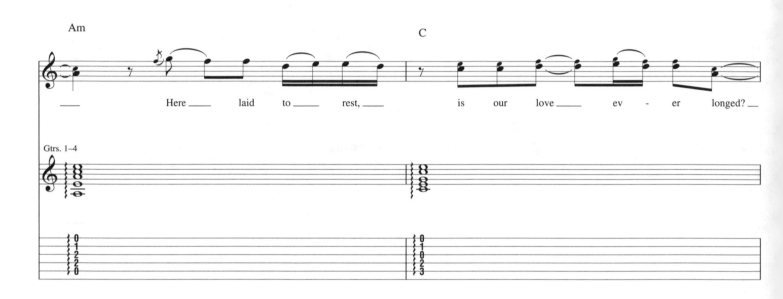

Gtr. 1 tacet

With truth ___ on the shores ___ of com - pas - sion.

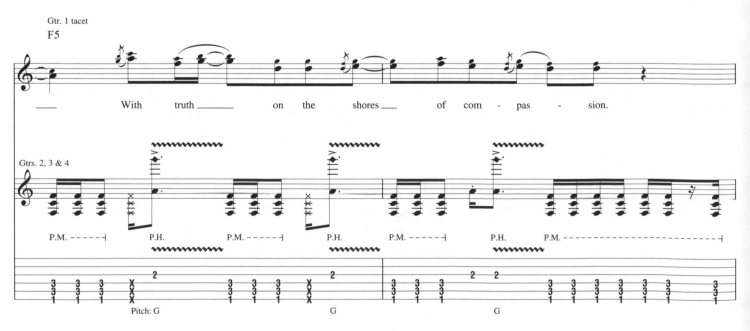

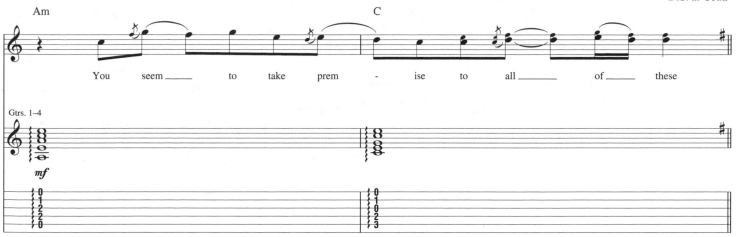

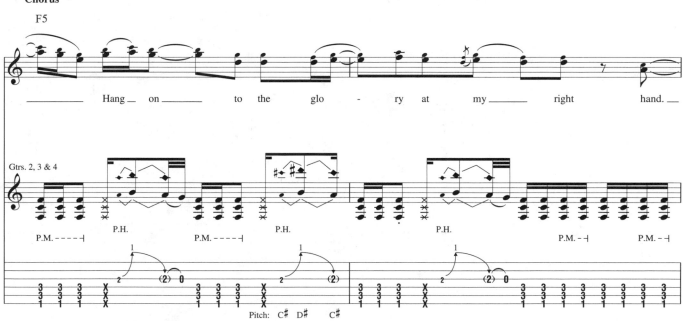

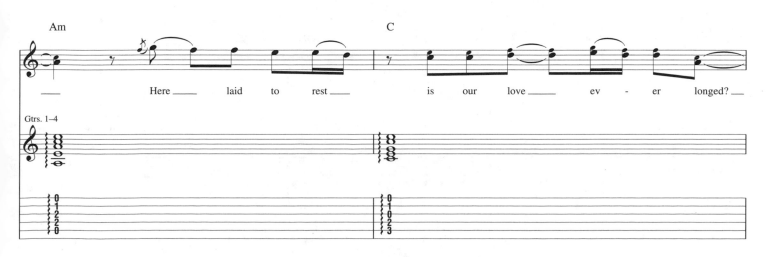

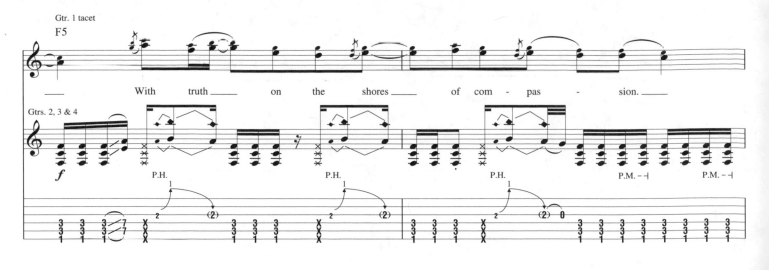

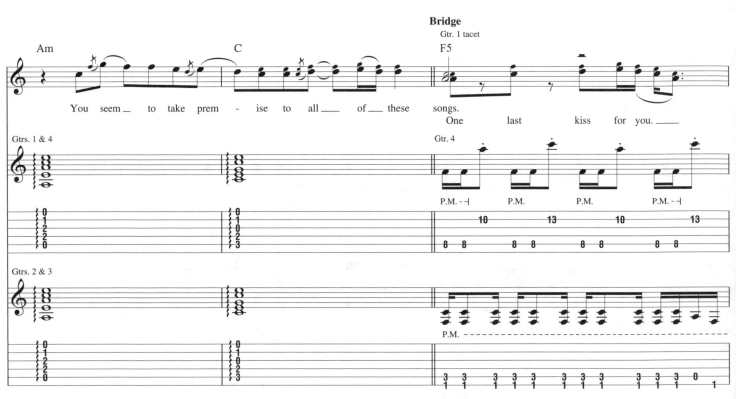

214

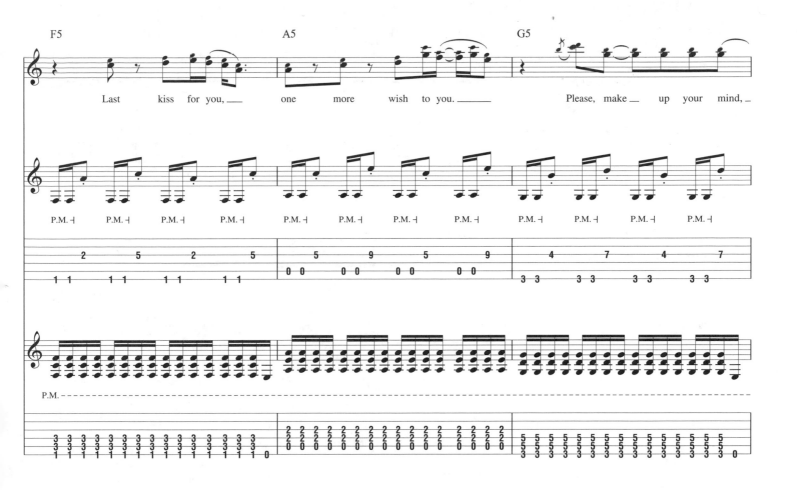

F5 · · · A5 · · · G5

Last kiss for you,___ one more wish to you.___ Please, make__ up your mind,__

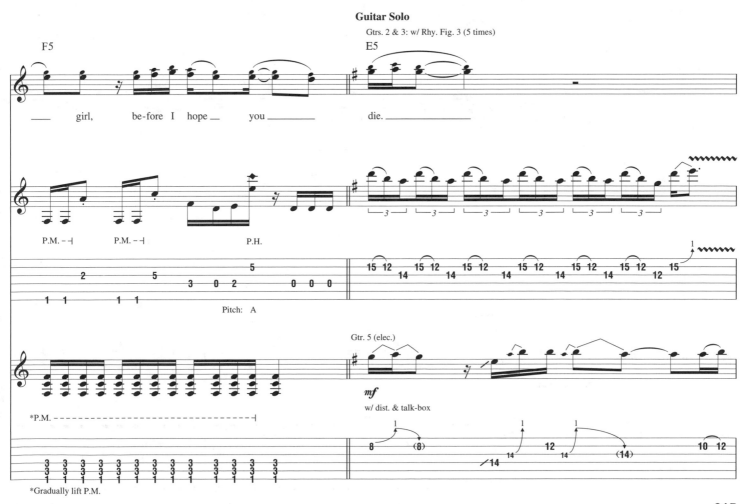

Guitar Solo

Gtrs. 2 & 3: w/ Rhy. Fig. 3 (5 times)

F5 · · · E5

___ girl, be-fore I hope__ you___ die.___

Pitch: A

Gtr. 5 (elec.)

mf

w/ dist. & talk-box

*Gradually lift P.M.

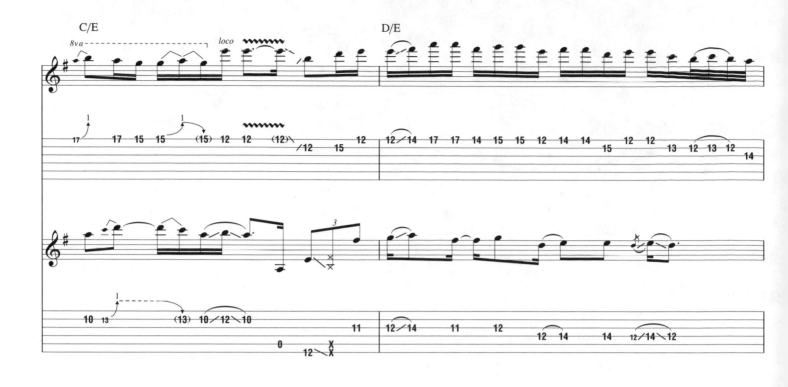

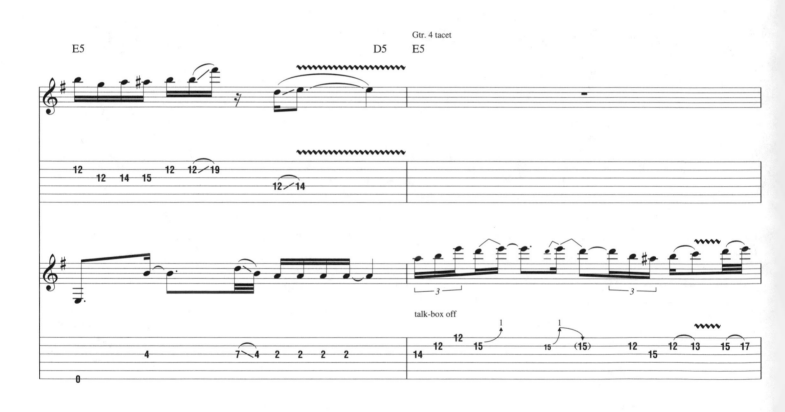

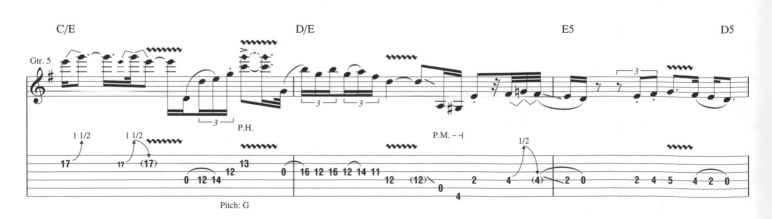

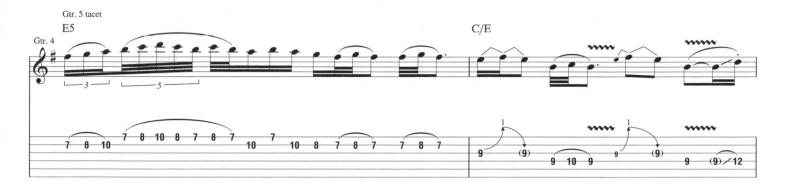

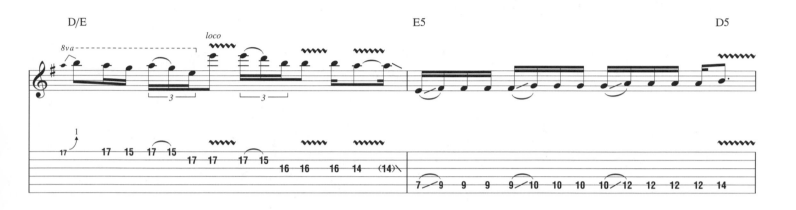

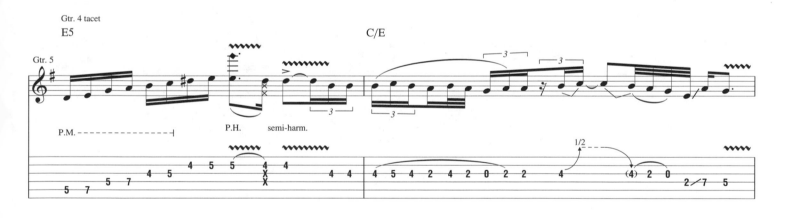

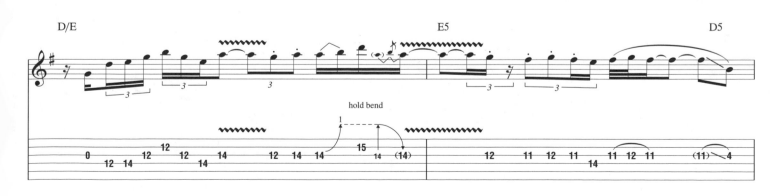

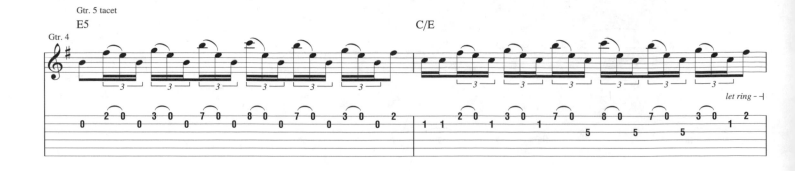

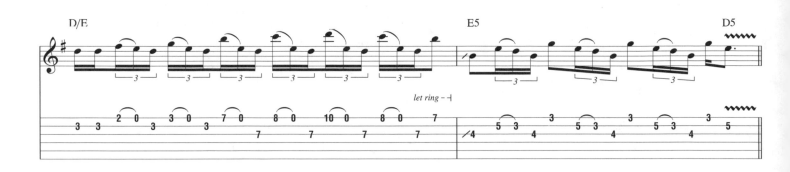

Outro

Gtrs. 2 & 3: w/ Rhy. Fig. 3 (till fade)
Gtr. 4 tacet

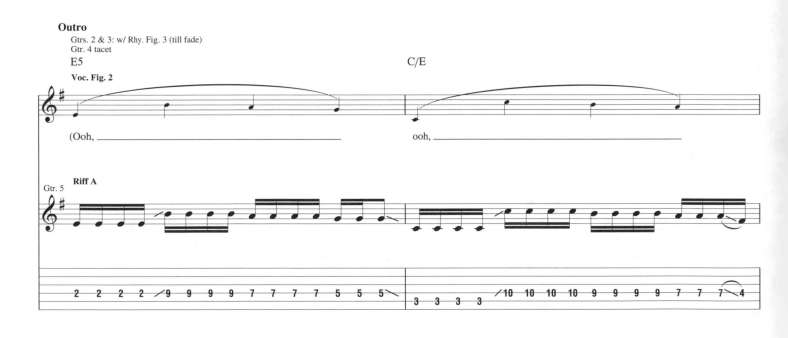

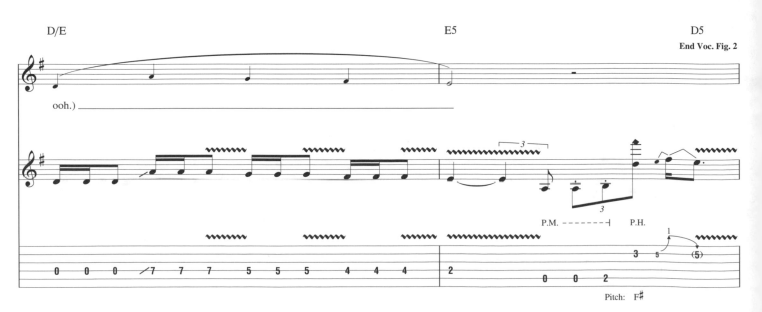

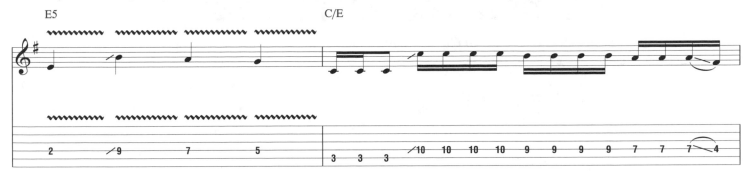

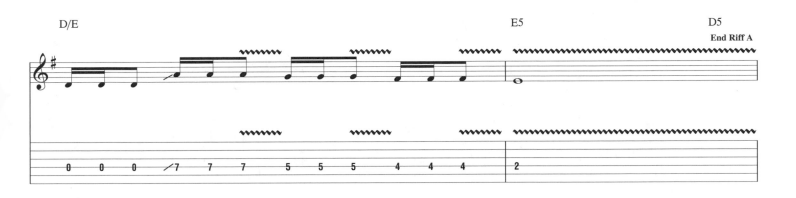

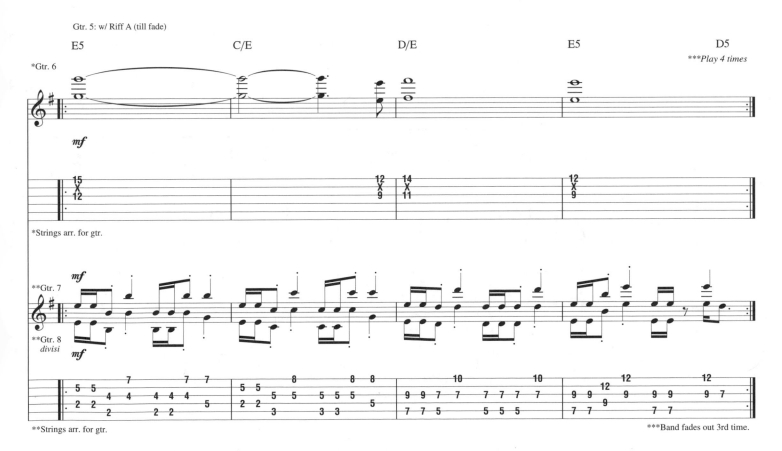

219

When You Were Young

Words and Music by Brandon Flowers, Dave Keuning, Mark Stoermer and Ronnie Vannucci

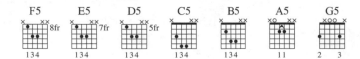

Tune down 1/2 step:
(low to high) Eb-Ab-Db-Gb-Bb-Eb

Intro

Moderately ♩ = 130

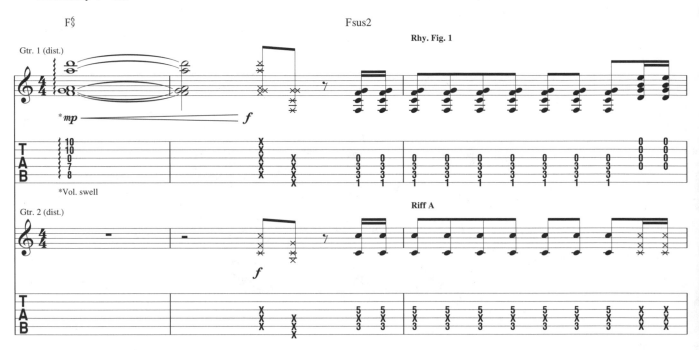

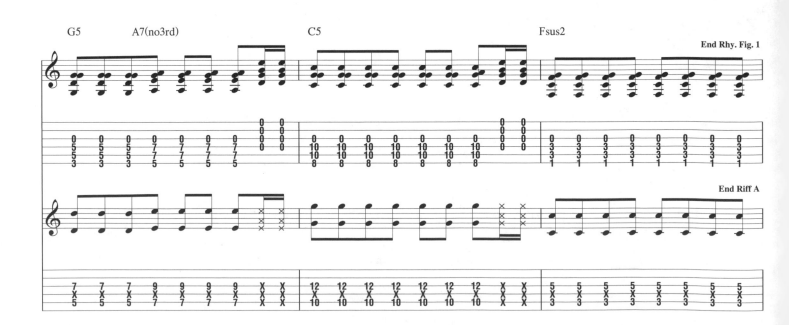

Gtr. 1: w/ Rhy. Fig. 1
Gtr. 2: w/ Riff A

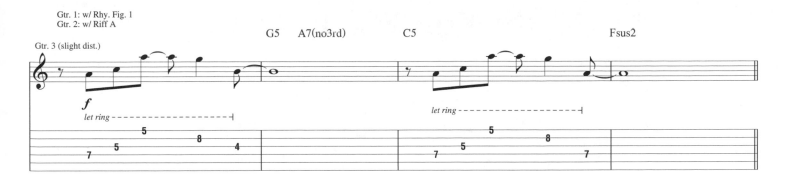

*Bass arr. for gtr.
**Chord symbols reflect implied harmony.
***Set for sixteenth-note regeneration w/ 6 repeats.

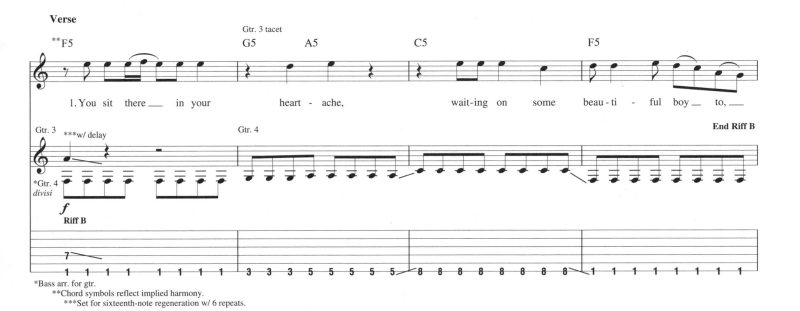

Gtr. 1: w/ Rhy. Fig. 1
Gtr. 2: w/ Riff A

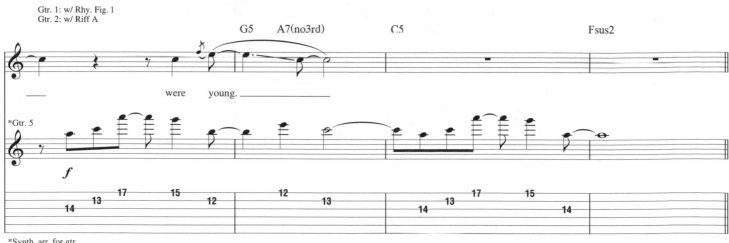

*Synth. arr. for gtr.

Verse

Gtr. 5 tacet

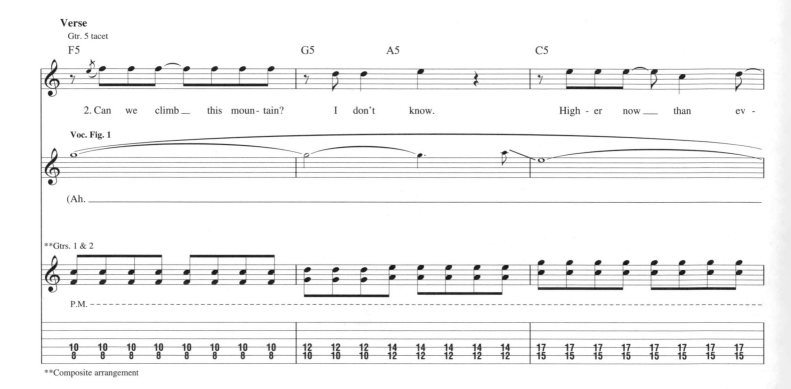

**Composite arrangement

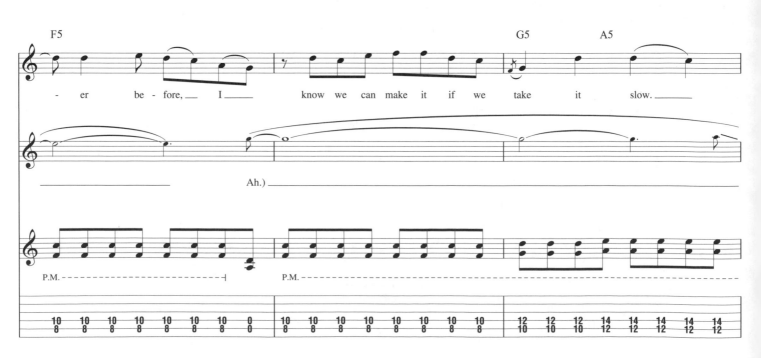

Verse

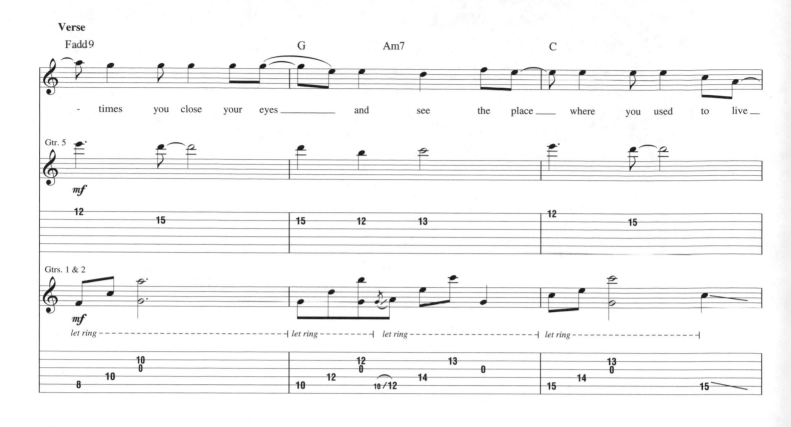

Lyrics: -times you close your eyes _____ and see the place _____ where you used to live _____

Interlude

Gtr. 1: w/ Rhy. Fig. 1 (2 times)
Gtr. 2: w/ Riff A (2 times)
Gtr. 5 tacet

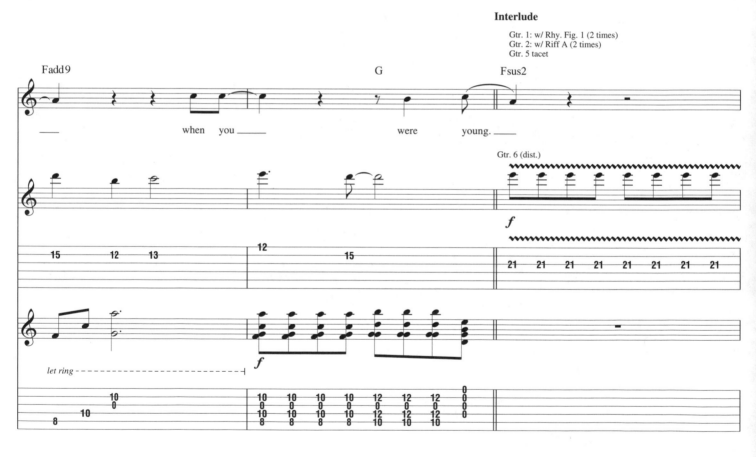

Lyrics: _____ when you _____ were young. _____

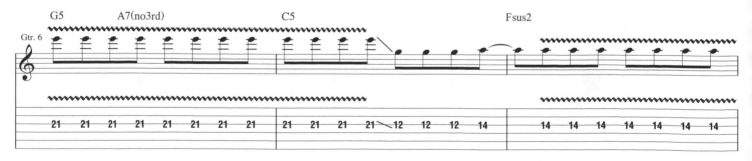

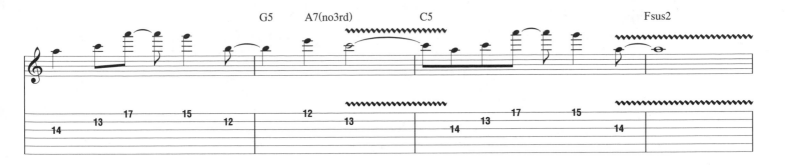

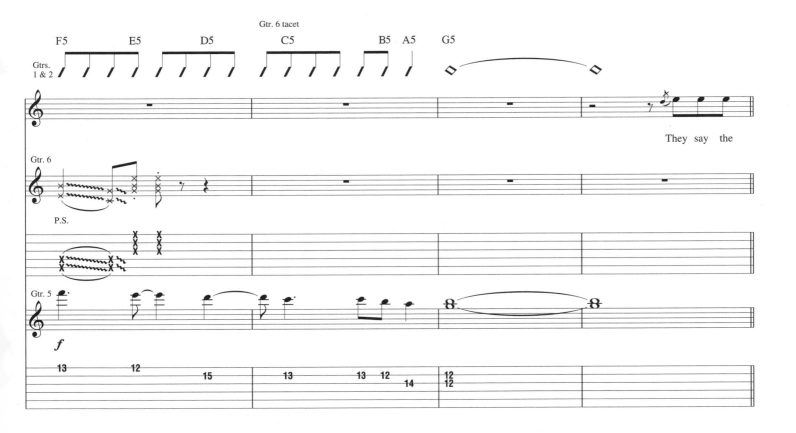

Gtr. 6 tacet

Bridge

Gtrs. 1 & 2 tacet

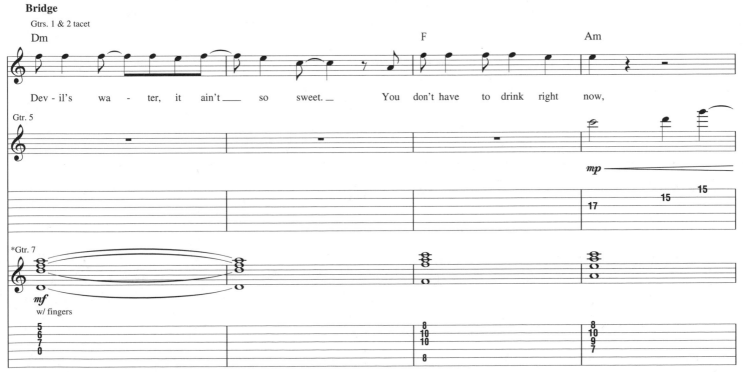

*Synth. arr. for gtr.

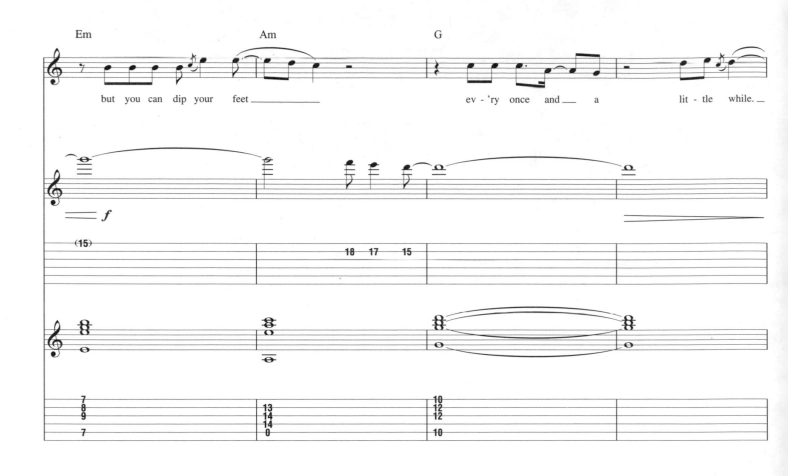

but you can dip your feet _____ ev - 'ry once and _ a lit - tle while. _

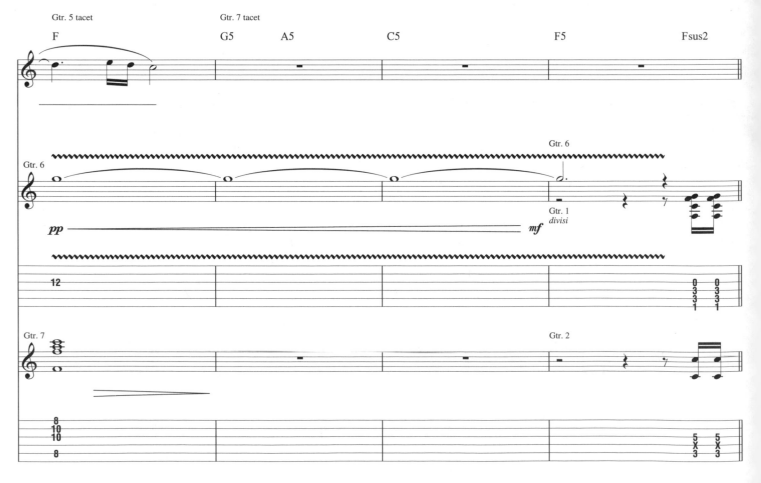

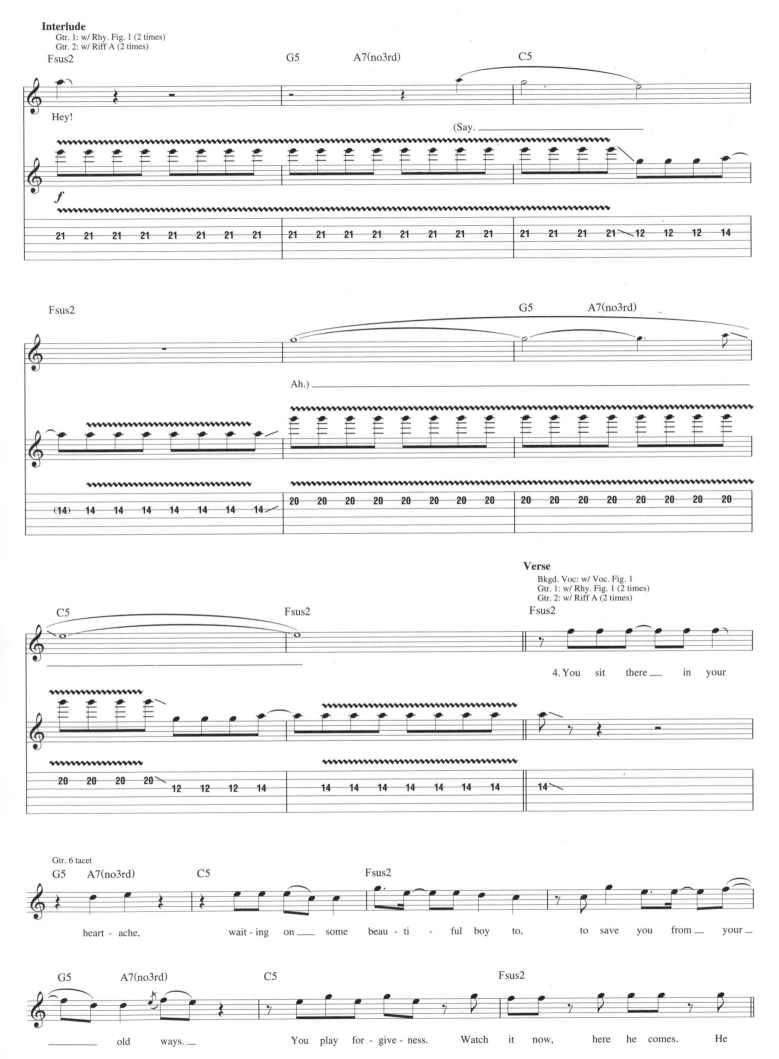

Outro-Chorus

doesn't look a thing like Je - sus ___ but he talks like a gen-tle-man, like you i - mag - ined when you

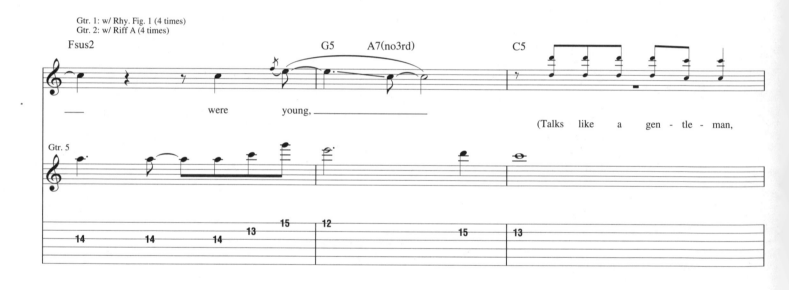

were young, ___ (Talks like a gen - tle - man,

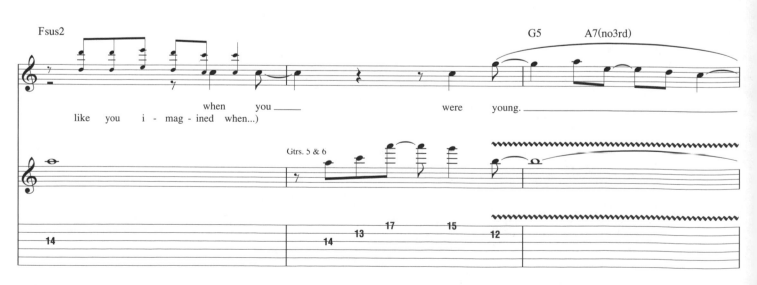

when you ___ were young. ___
like you i - mag - ined when...)

Won't Get Fooled Again

Words and Music by Pete Townshend

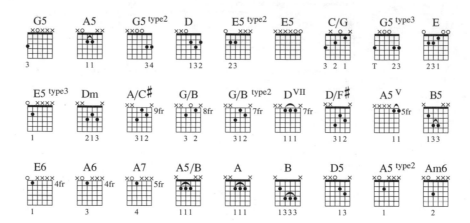

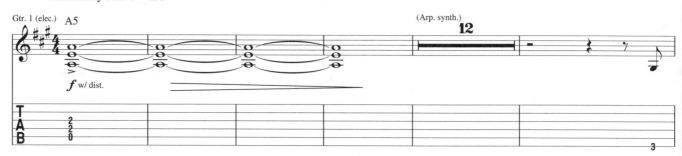

Intro

Moderately Fast ♩ = 136

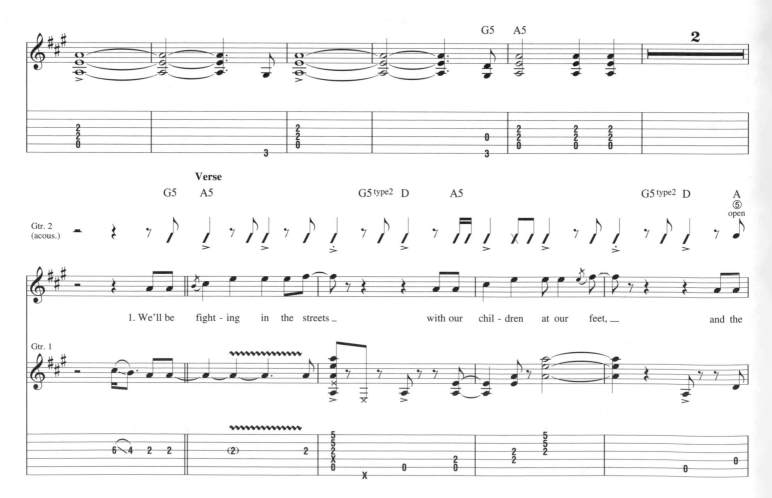

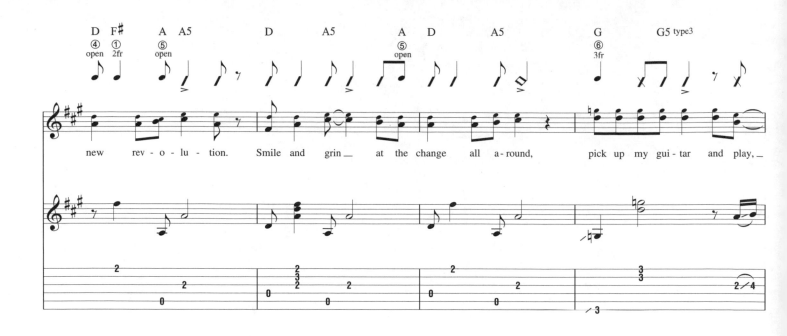

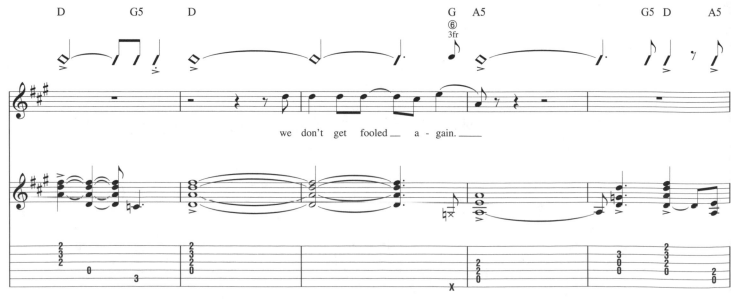

Chorus

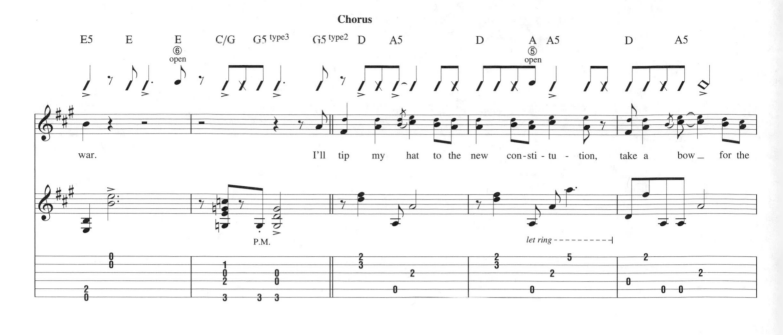

war.   I'll tip my hat to the new con-sti-tu-tion, take a bow _ for the

new rev-o-lu-tion. Smile and grin _ at the change all a-round,   pick up my gui-tar and play, _

_   just like yes-ter-day, _   then I'll get on   my knees and

pray   we don't get fooled _ a - gain. _____   No

pitch: D
*Harm. top note only.

no!

Gtr. 3 (elec.)

Gtr. 1

** Occasionally strike⑤ open (next 16 meas.)
† Mute strings by releasing finger pressure
(next 16 meas.)

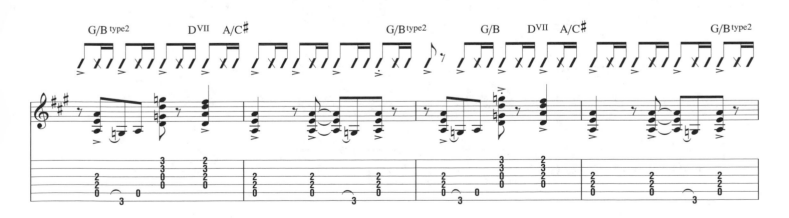

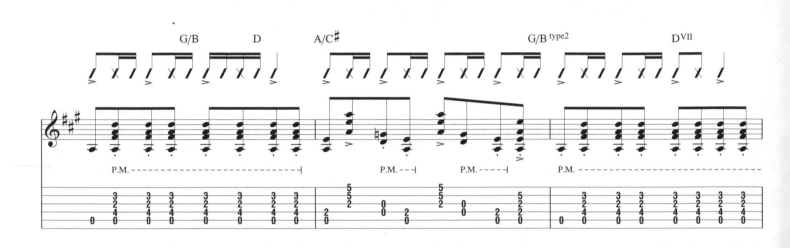

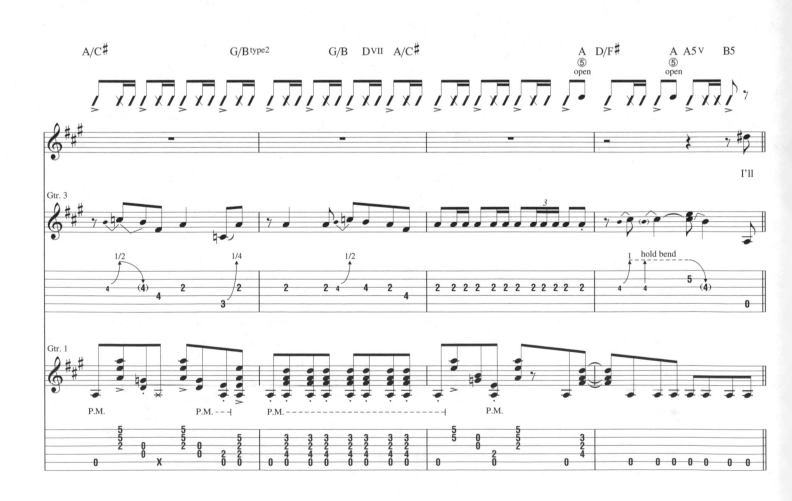

then I'll get on my knees and pray

we

don't get fooled _ a - gain. _____   Don't get fooled a - gain. _____   No, no!

*Played ahead of the beat

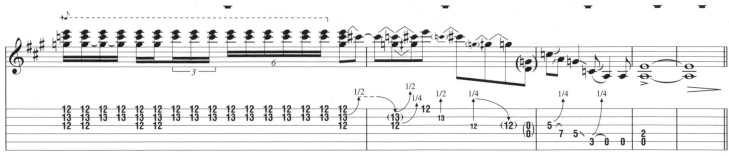

Interlude

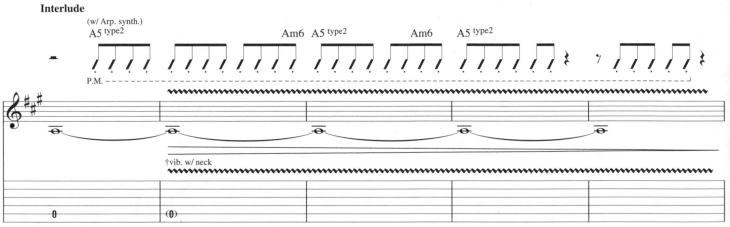

†Vibrato achieved by applying force with right hand on gtr. body & left hand on neck.

Outro

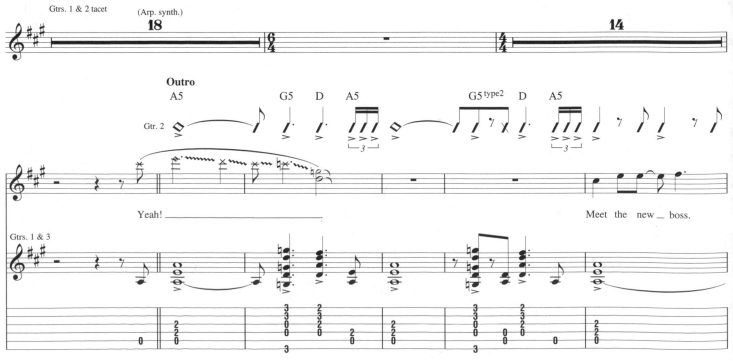

Same as the old boss.

Free Time

(Townshend:) Hey!

Guitar Notation Legend

Guitar music can be notated three different ways: on a *musical staff*, in *tablature*, and in *rhythm slashes*.

RHYTHM SLASHES are written above the staff. Strum chords in the rhythm indicated. Use the chord diagrams found at the top of the first page of the transcription for the appropriate chord voicings. Round noteheads indicate single notes.

THE MUSICAL STAFF shows pitches and rhythms and is divided by bar lines into measures. Pitches are named after the first seven letters of the alphabet.

TABLATURE graphically represents the guitar fingerboard. Each horizontal line represents a string, and each number represents a fret.

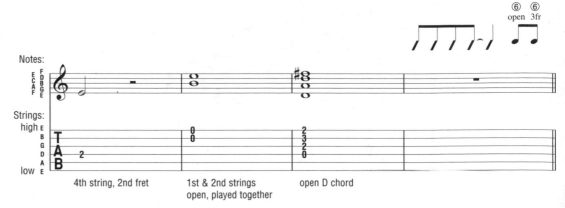

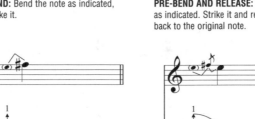

4th string, 2nd fret   1st & 2nd strings open, played together   open D chord

Definitions for Special Guitar Notation

HALF-STEP BEND: Strike the note and bend up 1/2 step.

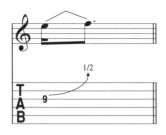

WHOLE-STEP BEND: Strike the note and bend up one step.

GRACE NOTE BEND: Strike the note and immediately bend up as indicated.

SLIGHT (MICROTONE) BEND: Strike the note and bend up 1/4 step.

BEND AND RELEASE: Strike the note and bend up as indicated, then release back to the original note. Only the first note is struck.

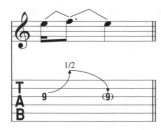

PRE-BEND: Bend the note as indicated, then strike it.

PRE-BEND AND RELEASE: Bend the note as indicated. Strike it and release the bend back to the original note.

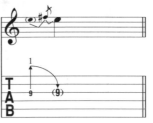

UNISON BEND: Strike the two notes simultaneously and bend the lower note up to the pitch of the higher.

VIBRATO: The string is vibrated by rapidly bending and releasing the note with the fretting hand.

WIDE VIBRATO: The pitch is varied to a greater degree by vibrating with the fretting hand.

HAMMER-ON: Strike the first (lower) note with one finger, then sound the higher note (on the same string) with another finger by fretting it without picking.

PULL-OFF: Place both fingers on the notes to be sounded. Strike the first note and without picking, pull the finger off to sound the second (lower) note.

LEGATO SLIDE: Strike the first note and then slide the same fret-hand finger up or down to the second note. The second note is not struck.

SHIFT SLIDE: Same as legato slide, except the second note is struck.

TRILL: Very rapidly alternate between the notes indicated by continuously hammering on and pulling off.

TAPPING: Hammer ("tap") the fret indicated with the pick-hand index or middle finger and pull off to the note fretted by the fret hand.

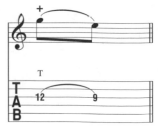

NATURAL HARMONIC: Strike the note while the fret-hand lightly touches the string directly over the fret indicated.

PINCH HARMONIC: The note is fretted normally and a harmonic is produced by adding the edge of the thumb or the tip of the index finger of the pick hand to the normal pick attack.

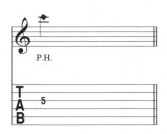

HARP HARMONIC: The note is fretted normally and a harmonic is produced by gently resting the pick hand's index finger directly above the indicated fret (in parentheses) while the pick hand's thumb or pick assists by plucking the appropriate string.

PICK SCRAPE: The edge of the pick is rubbed down (or up) the string, producing a scratchy sound.

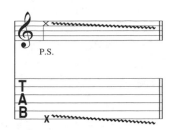

MUFFLED STRINGS: A percussive sound is produced by laying the fret hand across the string(s) without depressing, and striking them with the pick hand.

PALM MUTING: The note is partially muted by the pick hand lightly touching the string(s) just before the bridge.

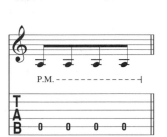

RAKE: Drag the pick across the strings indicated with a single motion.

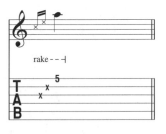

TREMOLO PICKING: The note is picked as rapidly and continuously as possible.

ARPEGGIATE: Play the notes of the chord indicated by quickly rolling them from bottom to top.

VIBRATO BAR DIVE AND RETURN: The pitch of the note or chord is dropped a specified number of steps (in rhythm), then returned to the original pitch.

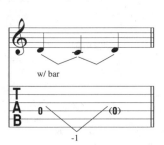

VIBRATO BAR SCOOP: Depress the bar just before striking the note, then quickly release the bar.

VIBRATO BAR DIP: Strike the note and then immediately drop a specified number of steps, then release back to the original pitch.

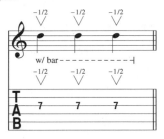

Additional Musical Definitions

(accent)	•	Accentuate note (play it louder).
(accent)	•	Accentuate note with great intensity.
(staccato)	•	Play the note short.
⊓	•	Downstroke
V	•	Upstroke

D.S. al Coda • Go back to the sign (𝄋), then play until the measure marked "*To Coda*," then skip to the section labelled "**Coda**."

D.C. al Fine • Go back to the beginning of the song and play until the measure marked "*Fine*" (end).

Rhy. Fig. • Label used to recall a recurring accompaniment pattern (usually chordal).

Riff • Label used to recall composed, melodic lines (usually single notes) which recur.

Fill • Label used to identify a brief melodic figure which is to be inserted into the arrangement.

Rhy. Fill • A chordal version of a Fill.

tacet • Instrument is silent (drops out).

• Repeat measures between signs.

• When a repeated section has different endings, play the first ending only the first time and the second ending only the second time.

NOTE: Tablature numbers in parentheses mean:
  1. The note is being sustained over a system (note in standard notation is tied), or
  2. The note is sustained, but a new articulation (such as a hammer-on, pull-off, slide or vibrato) begins, or
  3. The note is a barely audible "ghost" note (note in standard notation is also in parentheses).

RECORDED VERSIONS®
The Best Note-For-Note Transcriptions Available

ALL BOOKS INCLUDE TABLATURE

00692015 Aerosmith – Greatest Hits........................$22.95	00692931 Jimi Hendrix – Axis: Bold As Love $22.95	00694975 Queen – Greatest Hits $24.95
00690603 Aerosmith – O Yeah! (Ultimate Hits) $24.95	00690608 Jimi Hendrix – Blue Wild Angel.................$24.95	00690670 Queensryche – Very Best of.......................$19.95
00690178 Alice in Chains – Acoustic $19.95	00692932 Jimi Hendrix – Electric Ladyland...............$24.95	00690878 The Raconteurs – Broken Boy Soldiers $19.95
00694865 Alice in Chains – Dirt $19.95	00690017 Jimi Hendrix – Live at Woodstock $24.95	00694910 Rage Against the Machine..........................$19.95
00690387 Alice in Chains – Nothing Safe:	00690602 Jimi Hendrix – Smash Hits $19.95	00690055 Red Hot Chili Peppers –
The Best of the Box $19.95	00690843 H.I.M. – Dark Light $19.95	Blood Sugar Sex Magik $19.95
00690812 All American Rejects – Move Along............$19.95	00690869 Hinder – Extreme Behavior $19.95	00690584 Red Hot Chili Peppers – By the Way $19.95
00694932 Allman Brothers Band – Volume 1 ....$24.95	00690692 Billy Idol – Very Best of..........................$19.95	00690379 Red Hot Chili Peppers – Californication $19.95
00694933 Allman Brothers Band – Volume 2 ....$24.95	00690688 Incubus – A Crow Left of the Murder $19.95	00690673 Red Hot Chili Peppers – Greatest Hits $19.95
00694934 Allman Brothers Band – Volume 3 ....$24.95	00690457 Incubus – Make Yourself $19.95	00690852 Red Hot Chili Peppers –
00690865 Atreyu – A Deathgrip on Yesterday $19.95	00690544 Incubus – Morningview $19.95	Stadium Arcadium $24.95
00690609 Audioslave $19.95	00690790 Iron Maiden Anthology $24.95	00690511 Django Reinhardt – Definitive Collection....$19.95
00690804 Audioslave – Out of Exile $19.95	00690730 Alan Jackson – Guitar Collection $19.95	00690779 Relient K – MMHMM.............................$19.95
00690884 Audioslave – Revelations $19.95	00690721 Jet – Get Born $19.95	00690643 Relient K – Two Lefts Don't
00690820 Avenged Sevenfold – City of Evil $22.95	00690684 Jethro Tull – Aqualung $19.95	Make a Right...But Three Do $19.95
00690366 Bad Company – Original Anthology,	00690647 Jewel – Best of $19.95	00690631 Rolling Stones – Guitar Anthology.............$24.95
Book 1 ....$19.95	00690814 John5 – Songs for Sanity $19.95	00690685 David Lee Roth – Eat 'Em and Smile..........$19.95
00690503 Beach Boys – Very Best of $19.95	00690751 John5 – Vertigo $19.95	00690694 David Lee Roth – Guitar Anthology...........$24.95
00690489 Beatles – 1...$24.95	00690845 Eric Johnson – Bloom $19.95	00690031 Santana's Greatest Hits $19.95
00694929 Beatles – 1962-1966................................$24.95	00690846 Jack Johnson and Friends – Sing-A-Longs and	00690796 Michael Schenker – Very Best of...............$19.95
00694930 Beatles – 1967-1970................................$24.95	Lullabies for the Film Curious George $19.95	00690566 Scorpions – Best of...............................$19.95
00694832 Beatles – For Acoustic Guitar $22.95	00690271 Robert Johnson – New Transcriptions $24.95	00690604 Bob Seger – Guitar Collection $19.95
00690110 Beatles – White Album (Book 1) $19.95	00699131 Janis Joplin – Best of.............................$19.95	00690803 Kenny Wayne Shepherd Band – Best of $19.95
00692385 Chuck Berry $19.95	00690427 Judas Priest – Best of............................$19.95	00690857 Shinedown – Us and Them $19.95
00690835 Billy Talent $19.95	00690742 The Killers – Hot Fuss $19.95	00690530 Slipknot – Iowa $19.95
00692200 Black Sabbath –	00694903 Kiss – Best of.....................................$24.95	00690733 Slipknot – Vol. 3 (The Subliminal Verses)..$19.95
We Sold Our Soul for Rock 'N' Roll............$19.95	00690780 Korn – Greatest Hits, Volume 1 ....$22.95	00120004 Steely Dan – Best of...............................$24.95
00690674 blink-182 ....$19.95	00690834 Lamb of God – Ashes of the Wake $19.95	00694921 Steppenwolf – Best of............................$22.95
00690831 blink-182 – Greatest Hits $19.95	00690875 Lamb of God – Sacrament $19.95	00690655 Mike Stern – Best of..............................$19.95
00690491 David Bowie – Best of $19.95	00690823 Ray LaMontagne – Trouble $19.95	00690877 Stone Sour – Come What(ever) May $19.95
00690873 Breaking Benjamin – Phobia $19.95	00690679 John Lennon – Guitar Collection $19.95	00690520 Styx Guitar Collection $19.95
00690764 Breaking Benjamin – We Are Not Alone $19.95	00690781 Linkin Park – Hybrid Theory $22.95	00120081 Sublime $19.95
00690451 Jeff Buckley – Collection $24.95	00690782 Linkin Park – Meteora $22.95	00690771 SUM 41 – Chuck $19.95
00690590 Eric Clapton – Anthology.........................$29.95	00690783 Live – Best of $19.95	00690767 Switchfoot – The Beautiful Letdown $19.95
00690415 Clapton Chronicles – Best of Eric Clapton ..$18.95	00690743 Los Lonely Boys $19.95	00690830 System of a Down – Hypnotize $19.95
00690074 Eric Clapton – The Cream of Clapton $24.95	00690876 Los Lonely Boys – Sacred $19.95	00690799 System of a Down – Mezmerize $19.95
00690716 Eric Clapton – Me and Mr. Johnson $19.95	00690720 Lostprophets – Start Something................$19.95	00690531 System of a Down – Toxicity $19.95
00694869 Eric Clapton – Unplugged $22.95	00694954 Lynyrd Skynyrd – New Best of.................$19.95	00694824 James Taylor – Best of...........................$16.95
00690162 The Clash – Best of $19.95	00690752 Lynyrd Skynyrd – Street Survivors............$19.95	00690871 Three Days Grace – One-X $19.95
00690828 Coheed & Cambria I'm Burning	00690577 Yngwie Malmsteen – Anthology...............$24.95	00690737 3 Doors Down – The Better Life $22.95
Star, IV, Vol. 1: From Fear Through the	00690754 Marilyn Manson – Lest We Forget $19.95	00690683 Robin Trower – Bridge of Sighs $19.95
Eyes of Madness $19.95	00694956 Bob Marley– Legend $19.95	00690740 Shania Twain – Guitar Collection $19.95
00690593 Coldplay – A Rush of Blood to the Head.....$19.95	00694945 Bob Marley– Songs of Freedom $24.95	00699191 U2 – Best of: 1980-1990 ....$19.95
00690838 Cream – Royal Albert Hall:	00690657 Maroon5 – Songs About Jane $19.95	00690732 U2 – Best of: 1990-2000 ....$19.95
London May 2-3-5-6 2005 ....$22.95	00120080 Don McLean – Songbook $19.95	00690775 U2 – How to Dismantle an Atomic Bomb ...$22.95
00690856 Creed – Greatest Hits $22.95	00694951 Megadeth – Rust in Peace $22.95	00690575 Steve Vai – Alive in an Ultra World $22.95
00690401 Creed – Human Clay $19.95	00690768 Megadeth – The System Has Failed............$19.95	00660137 Steve Vai – Passion & Warfare $24.95
00690819 Creedence Clearwater Revival – Best of $19.95	00690505 John Mellencamp – Guitar Collection.........$19.95	00691116 Stevie Ray Vaughan – Guitar Collection $24.95
00690572 Steve Cropper – Soul Man $19.95	00690646 Pat Metheny – One Quiet Night $19.95	00660058 Stevie Ray Vaughan –
00690613 Crosby, Stills & Nash – Best of $19.95	00690558 Pat Metheny – Trio: 99>00 ....$19.95	Lightnin' Blues 1983-1987.......................$24.95
00690289 Deep Purple – Best of $17.95	00690040 Steve Miller Band – Young Hearts $19.95	00694835 Stevie Ray Vaughan – The Sky Is Crying $22.95
00690784 Def Leppard – Best of $19.95	00690794 Mudvayne – Lost and Found $19.95	00690015 Stevie Ray Vaughan – Texas Flood $19.95
00690347 The Doors – Anthology............................$22.95	00690611 Nirvana $22.95	00690772 Velvet Revolver – Contraband $22.95
00690348 The Doors – Essential Guitar Collection $16.95	00694883 Nirvana – Nevermind $19.95	00690071 Weezer (The Blue Album) $19.95
00690810 Fall Out Boy – From Under the Cork Tree ...$19.95	00690026 Nirvana – Unplugged in New York $19.95	00690447 The Who – Best of................................$24.95
00690664 Fleetwood Mac – Best of $19.95	00690807 The Offspring – Greatest Hits $19.95	00690589 ZZ Top Guitar Anthology........................$22.95
00690870 Flyleaf $19.95	00694847 Ozzy Osbourne – Best of $22.95	
00690808 Foo Fighters – In Your Honor $19.95	00690399 Ozzy Osbourne – Ozzman Cometh.............$19.95	
00690805 Robben Ford – Best of $19.95	00690866 Panic! At the Disco –	
00694920 Free – Best of.......................................$19.95	A Fever You Can't Sweat Out $19.95	
00690848 Godsmack – IV $19.95	00694855 Pearl Jam – Ten $19.95	
00690601 Good Charlotte –	00690439 A Perfect Circle – Mer De Noms $19.95	
The Young and the Hopeless $19.95	00690661 A Perfect Circle – Thirteenth Step.............$19.95	
00690697 Jim Hall – Best of $19.95	00690499 Tom Petty – Definitive Guitar Collection $19.95	
00690840 Ben Harper – Both Sides of the Gun $19.95	00690428 Pink Floyd – Dark Side of the Moon $19.95	
00694798 George Harrison – Anthology....................$19.95	00690789 Poison – Best of...................................$19.95	
00692930 Jimi Hendrix – Are You Experienced?.........$24.95	00693864 The Police – Best of..............................$19.95	